Dedication

To Margaret Chisholm
July 25, 1921 – November 21, 1999
Her motto: "Motivate, inspire, and lead."

Contents

Figure List

Preface

Many college research and writing assignments require students to locate, select, and evaluate information. In order to do this successfully, it is critical that they understand how to use the increasing number of information resources and technologies efficiently and effectively.

The essential tools of my university study in the United States were *Webster's Collegiate Dictionary*, *Roget's Thesaurus*, Strunk and White's *Elements of Style,* and Kate Turabian's *Manual for Writers of Term Papers, Theses, and Dissertations.* The only item I sorely lacked was a book to tell me where and how to look up other information when I needed it.

Perhaps this lack is what led me to become a librarian. After many years in the field, I decided to write a guide to fill that need. I hope this book becomes an essential tool of the knowledgeable student.

Techniques for Student Research is designed to help students develop their searching skills. It can be used as a personal "how to" guide or as a text for an introductory course on information and research skills. Students can either read the book straight through or consult appropriate chapters as required. Topics are cross referenced to related topics in other chapters, and there is a comprehensive index. The primary focus is on the information needs and interests of undergraduate students. However, high school students taking advanced placement classes or graduate students who need to review the basics of information searching will also find this book helpful.

Information is presented in an informal style that is easy to read and understand. The goal is to motivate students to discover and use a wide range of information sources, and help them gain confidence and competence in their manual and online searching strategies.

The first part of the book (Chapters 2 to 9) covers the basics of using printed and electronic reference sources to find short, factual answers to questions. It does not provide long lists and descriptions of these reference sources; instead, it emphasizes the principles of organization and searching techniques that apply to particular types, such as dictionaries, encyclopedias, and maps and atlases. The aim is to give students the confidence to determine the type of resource they need, select from those available, and use them competently.

The second part of the book (Chapters 10 to 20) covers the research process—formulating a search strategy to answer complex questions requiring analysis of information from a variety of sources. Each step of the search strategy is presented clearly and illustrated with examples. Again, emphasis is on the principles and techniques that apply across a range of printed and electronic sources. Students are also encouraged to explore beyond their own college library by consulting experts and using other library collections and information services as appropriate.

The final chapter provides a brief introduction to the Internet, which will help students to use the Internet resources that have been referred to throughout the book. The appendices provide further assistance with alphabetical arrangement and book-related terminology.

Because the "information landscape" is constantly changing and resources quickly become outdated, this book emphasizes the processes rather than particular publications or websites. Students are shown techniques for locating the most appropriate resources—resources that may not even have existed when this book was being written!

This book is a collaborative effort of three persons: Dr. Nancy Lane, Dr. Margaret Chisholm, and Carolyn Mateer. Nancy grew up in the United States, but moved to Australia where she wrote this book. It is now in its second edition and used widely by university students there. Nancy was the head of the Centre for Library and Information Studies at the University of Canberra, and is now the development officer at the Australian Academy of Science.

Margaret and Carolyn adapted the book for use in the United States. Margaret was the director of the Graduate School of Library and Information Science and Carolyn was the head of Reference and Research Services at the University of Washington.

The writers appreciate the assistance of the following librarians from the University of Washington Libraries who offered many helpful suggestions: Cynthia Blanding, Access Services; Eleanor Chase, Government Publications; Glenda Pearson, Microforms-Newspapers Librarian; Carla Rickerson, Pacific Northwest Collection; Mary Wishner, Law Library; and Kathryn Womble, Map Collection.

We hope that this book will prove as useful to American students as it has for thousands of Australian students. Finding the information they need should become both an enjoyable and rewarding task.

1

Information Content, Information Packages

Information is what we need to know, when we need to know it. It may be one word in answer to a simple question, such as "What time is it?" or "What's the weather like?". Or it may be contained in a wide range of books, journals, and computer databases that help to provide answers to complex research questions, such as "What causes cancer?" or "Why did dinosaurs become extinct?". If we are to find and use information efficiently, however, we must define the concept more precisely.

WHAT IS INFORMATION?

First and foremost, information is *content*—the meaning conveyed, regardless of how it is communicated. Although computers are becoming more and more important in our society, they are just one means of storing and transmitting information; there are many others. Information is a broader concept than information technology.

It is useful to think of information as part of a continuum: Data → Information → Knowledge → Understanding → Communication.

Data are facts and figures, based on observation, surveys, or research, that have been collected and are available for use. *Information* consists of data that have been organized

1

for the potential benefit of individuals. *Knowledge* is information that individuals recognize as relevant and think about and interpret, thereby gaining *understanding*. They may also use this understanding for a purpose, which usually involves *communication*.

Information literacy is the capacity to know when you need information, what sort you need, where to find it, and how to evaluate and organize it. A report by the American Library Association identified information literacy as essential for critical thinking. In reviewing this report, Breivik noted (1991: 226): "It does not matter how well people can analyze or synthesize; if they do not start with an adequate, accurate, and up-to-date body of information, they will not come up with a good answer."

The ability to access, retrieve, and evaluate information could even be considered part of the definition of literacy itself. As Breivik and Gee stated (1989: 23): "In an era when today's 'truths' become tomorrow's outdated concepts, individuals who are unable to gather pertinent information are almost as helpless as those who are unable to read or write."

WHY DO WE NEED INFORMATION?

Some writers have said that information is the raw material used in the decision-making process; others, that it is a basic ingredient of social, personal, technological, and political change. One government report stated that information is central to economic production, education, welfare, arts, and the media. It enables citizens to participate fully in society—to access services, act on opportunities, and make informed decisions about their lives. It is essential in promoting social justice for all.

Put more personally and simply, information is useful to you every day. It can help you find a satisfactory place to live, eat nutritious food, stay healthy, study and learn effectively, communicate with family and friends, make judicious purchases, work constructively, live in harmony with the environment, participate in sports and hobbies, elect people to govern, understand world events, and appreciate culture. It can amuse, encourage, motivate, cheer, and inspire you.

In this book, the focus on information is much narrower, however. Emphasis is on the processes needed for locating information essential for writing essays, preparing class presentations, and passing exams, as well as for pursuing personal interests.

INFORMATION PACKAGES

Information content may be packaged in many different ways to cater to the needs of particular users at particular times. Let's take a simple example. To find out the time, you can look at your watch, dial TIME on the telephone, ask a friend, turn on the radio and listen to the announcer, or check the position of the sun in the sky. Although the information content is always the same, each of these information packages is different.

Each *information package* is determined by the *medium* (the physical form of communication) and the *format* (the particular means of presenting the information), combined with any unique characteristics common to that package. These concepts are explained more fully in Chapter 12.

Now let's look at the hypothetical development of the solar barbecue in Figure 1–1. In this example you can see how information has been created and communicated in a variety of different packages over time. Each stage in the process follows logically.

Figure 1–1 The variety of information packages created and communicated in the hypothetical development of the solar barbecue.

Process	Package
Andy, a budding inventor, says to his friends one afternoon over a few beers: "It's too hot to be lighting the barbecue. We should be using the sun to cook a few steaks."	Personal conversation
He thinks about the idea for a few weeks, then telephones a designer for help.	Telephone conversation Technical drawing
Andy builds a small-scale replica to see that it works, and takes out a patent.	Model Patent
He writes a business plan for his bank manager to get the money to go into production and negotiates the manufacture with a local firm.	Report Legal contract
Andy invites his friends to the launch of the first solar barbecue off the production line.	E-mail message Letter
Andy's children take a video of Dad in apron and chef's hat cooking a hot dog to commemorate the event.	Video recording
Andy's wife takes slides of the barbecue in action to use in his advertising literature.	35-mm transparency Brochure

Figure 1–1 *Continued*	
Process	**Package**
The daily newspaper sends out a reporter and photographer to cover the story, and the local radio station broadcasts an interview.	Newspaper Photograph Radio program
Andy is asked to speak at the Inventor's Conference and his talk is recorded for sale to the participants.	Conference Reel-to-reel tape recording Audiocassette
He writes a technical article describing his design for the *Solar Journal*. The article is indexed, and the citation is available on CD-ROM and online.	Journal CD-ROM Online computer access
The solar barbecue becomes popular and the Department of Agriculture publishes a book of recipes called *Barbecuing Solar.*	Book
Andy's fame spreads. He appears on the television evening news cooking a steak for the governor after the baseball playoffs.	Television program
Andy retires a millionaire and donates his papers and documents to the state library for posterity.	Manuscript Archival material

If you are seeking information about solar barbecues, however, you would not normally be aware of all these steps in the process of information production. The total amount of information available would also be irrelevant. You would want just enough to answer your question or solve your problem, and to get it in the easiest way possible.

SEARCHING FOR INFORMATION

With such a plethora of information potentially available, how can you find the right amount, in the most appropriate package, as quickly as possible? The process of searching for information can be intricate and sometimes tedious, but it can be broken down into basic steps that make it seem easier.

The first step is to categorize your information requirement by complexity. If you want a simple, straightforward, factual answer likely to be found in one well-chosen information source, then yours is a *reference query* (or "ready reference" query in the jargon of librarians). If, however, you want to understand and explain a complex concept, process, or event that requires searching out, analyzing, synthesizing, and interpreting material from a range of information sources, then yours is a *research query*. Figure 1–2 gives a quick test for deciding between these two types of queries.

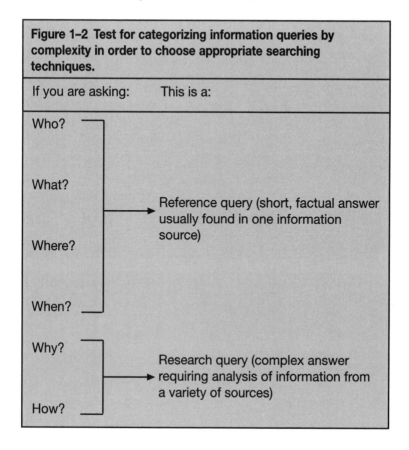

Figure 1–2 Test for categorizing information queries by complexity in order to choose appropriate searching techniques.

Chapters 2 through 9 in this book discuss sources and techniques for dealing with reference queries, and Chapters 10 through 20 discuss those for dealing with research queries. Chapter 21 briefly describes the Internet, which can provide information on both types of queries.

2

Reference Works: Finding Facts Fast

Reference works are not intended to be read through from start to finish, but to be consulted when needed. They are of two types: those that contain actual information and those that lead to other sources containing the information. To avoid confusion, we will call the first type *reference works* and the second type *finding aids*.

Reference works are used to answer reference queries asking "Who?," "What?," "Where?," or "When?". Finding aids are used for locating information sources to answer research queries asking "Why?" or "How?". Finding aids are discussed briefly in Chapter 14 and in detail in Chapters 17 to 20.

Many types of reference works are now available in electronic as well as printed form. For example, dictionaries and thesauruses may come as part of standard word-processing software. Encyclopedias are available on CD-ROM, and numerous directories can be consulted on the Internet. This chapter deals first with printed and then electronic reference works.

PRINTED REFERENCE WORKS

All printed reference works have four essential features. Once you can analyze these features and understand their interrelationship, you will be able to use any printed reference work whether you have seen it before or not. The four essential features are:

- number and types of lists of entries
- order of arrangement within the lists
- access to the lists
- data elements included in each entry.

Let's look at these features in detail, with some examples to make them clear.

Lists of Entries

If you browse through any printed reference work, you will usually find one or two main lists of entries. A dictionary, for example, has a list of words. A telephone directory has a list of people and business firms by name (the *White Pages*), and a list of business firms by products and services (the *Yellow Pages*).

There may be more than one or two lists of entries. A dictionary may also have separate lists of geographic features, names of prominent people, or new words added just before publication. A telephone directory may have separate lists for emergency assistance, local government, community services, or area codes.

Over time, rules of thumb have developed for the order in which these lists normally appear. In dictionaries, for example, the main list of words is usually at the beginning, with shorter lists at the back as appendices. In the *White Pages* the lists of area codes, government agencies, and community services usually precede the main list of personal and business names.

Order of Arrangement

Each of these lists of entries is arranged in sequence by the *entry headings*. The four most important orders of arrangement are:

- alphabetical
- numerical or chronological
- spatial
- classified.

The most common order of arrangement is *alphabetical*—dictionaries and telephone directories are arranged this way. There are variations in alphabetical order, however, and these are explained in Appendix 1.

Lists of entries with a *numerical* order of arrangement are often found in almanacs. They may include widely diverse topics, from chemical elements and their attributes by atomic number (1: hydrogen, 2: helium, . . .), to gifts by wedding anniversaries (1st: cotton, . . . 50th: gold, . . .). Almanacs, as well as yearbooks and news digest services, may use *chronological* orders of arrangement, particularly for lists of historical events (for example, Nobel Prize winners by year).

Atlases, map series, and street directories rely on a *spatial* order of arrangement—that is, a grid pattern imposed on a mapped area as a whole, with the resulting divisions presented as enlargements.

In a *classified* order of arrangement the content of a list is organized according to the unique characteristics of the field covered. For example, *Roget's Thesaurus* arranges the words in the English language by similarities in their meanings. Field guides may be arranged by botanical or zoological classification schemes: kingdom, phylum, class, order, family, genus, and species.

A reference work that uses an unusual classified order of arrangement is *Mushrooms of North America* by Alan Bessette and Walter J. Sundberg, where species are arranged based on similarities in their shape and form. Illustrations are provided for identification by cap, cap edge, spacing of gills, and stalk. The form descriptions and names do capture attention: Under "Mushrooms with a ring and cup" are listed "Destroying Angel," "Death Cap," "Yellow Patches," and "Blusher."

Reference works with a classified order of arrangement may use letters, numbers, colors, or other symbols as a code to represent the topics, and the sequencing of this code is specifically defined or described. Usually, however, it incorporates some type of alphabetical or numerical arrangement. *Roget's Thesaurus*, for example, uses a numerical system of three digits, a period, and one or two more digits.

Depending on the amount of duplication among entry headings, some lists may also have a subsidiary order of arrangement. In the *White Pages*, for example, all persons having an identical surname and initials may be listed alphabetically by suburb. In a gazetteer, all towns and cities of the same name may be listed alphabetically by state or country.

Access to the Lists of Entries

To find the information you want in a printed reference work, you need to locate the right entry in the right list. To do this, you must use an appropriate *access term*—that is, any word or phrase by which an entry containing the information can be located.

In many printed reference works, such as dictionaries, biographical dictionaries, and the *White Pages* of telephone directories, the only access terms are the entry headings. If an entry does not appear under the expected heading, you will need to think of an alternative access term (that is, another likely heading). For example, if you are looking up the author Mark Twain in a biographical dictionary but can't find him, you'll have to think up the alternative—his real name, Samuel Clemens.

Figure 2–1 Examples of types of "see" references.

Ca. See Calcium. (Abbreviation to whole word)

Collar bone. See Clavicle. (Common to scientific name)

Czar. See Tsar. (Variant spelling)

Mice. See Mouse. (Irregular plural to singular)

Soapstone. See Talc. (Synonym)

Strategic Arms Limitation Talks. See SALT. (Full name to acronym)

Stratton, Charles. See Tom Thumb. (Real name to pseudonym)

Television, closed circuit. See Closed circuit television. (Inverted to normal word order)

Van Gogh, Vincent. See Gogh, Vincent Van. (Parts of compound surname)

Some printed reference works may be more helpful. Their compilers know that users may be looking for an entry using a word that is different, but that means the same, as the entry heading. These other words are also included as access terms, arranged in their proper order in the list of entries with a brief note telling users which heading to go to in order to find the entry. These notes are called *"see" references* or *cross references*.

These additional access terms may be related to the entry headings in a number of ways, and several examples are shown in Figure 2–1. This approach is used in many encyclopedias, particularly the one- or two-volume sets.

Sometimes the arrangement of entries in a list may not be obvious to users. Such sources rely on *indexes*—separate, supplementary lists of access terms that guide users to the right entry. *Roget's Thesaurus*, with its classified arrangement, and most almanacs and handbooks use this approach.

In essence, an index functions like a list of entries in miniature. Most often, the entries consist of the access term (often called an *index term*) used as the heading, followed by the location of the entry. The location may be a page number (for example, "Ireland, 452"), entry number ("Population control, 2057"), classification code and entry number ("Ozone depletion C7–1006"), or the entry heading used ("Total quality management, See TQM").

Sometimes compilers of reference works may also want to let users know that there are entries which, while not on the exact topic referred to by the access term, may be worth pursuing. In this case, in addition to giving the location for the entry on the topic, the index may suggest other entries to look under. These are called *"see also" references* (for example: "Space shuttles, pp. 403–412 [photos]. See also Launch vehicles; Spacecraft").

Data Elements

Each entry in a list provides a description or explanation of a particular topic, set out in a consistent way. The description or explanation (in effect, the information) is composed of *data elements*: words, phrases, sentences, or paragraphs, even pages, each devoted to a particular aspect of the topic.

We've already mentioned the entry heading—the data element at the beginning of the entry, by which the entry is assigned a sequential place in the list. In a dictionary, for example, the word being defined is the heading, and other data elements may include pronunciation, definitions, and derivation.

The way an entry is set out is usually standardized for each list, and often across all the lists in a reference work. It is determined by the:

- *data set*, or the number and type of data elements provided for each entry
- *set order*, or the sequence in which the data elements are presented

- *style*, that is, the indentation, typeface, punctuation, capitalization, and so on used for each entry.

An entry in the *White Pages* of a telephone directory, for example, may comprise a data set of five elements: name as the heading, street address, suburb, ZIP code, and telephone number, in that set order. The style may require the surname to be in bold and to precede the first name or initials; the street address to follow immediately; the suburb, ZIP code, and telephone number to be right justified and separated from the other data elements by a dashed line, with the telephone number in bold.

USING PRINTED REFERENCE WORKS

How do you go about analyzing these four essential features when you use a reference work for the first time? Your first step is to look in the table of contents, or scan the spines of a multi-volume work, to see the number and types of lists of entries. This is particularly important for reference works that you do not use regularly. For example, a Navajo language dictionary may have a list of phrases as well as a list of words. A film resource guide may have four separate lists: directors, production companies, equipment suppliers, and film-rental firms.

Your second step is to check how the entries in the lists are arranged. If they are alphabetical, you can search directly in the appropriate list for your access term or use the index as an intermediate step to locate it. If you are not successful, try alternative access terms of the types indicated in Figure 2–1.

If the order of arrangement is numerical, spatial, or classified, you may have to use an index. Although indexes are usually listed in the table of contents, you may just want to flip to the back and see what there is. Indexes to reference works are usually by subject, but there may also be separate indexes by authors of items cited, literary characters, geographical features, chemical elements, and so on. If you can understand everything in the entry once you find it, fine. If not, your next step is to check the introduction, foreword, preface, appendices, or inside covers of the reference work to find:

- a sample entry, explanation, or key to the contents of an entry
- a list of the abbreviations used in the reference work.

These will help you to unscramble an entry or interpret the information provided.

If you decide to make use of any of the information from a printed reference work, your final step is to take down all the relevant publishing details. This step is discussed in Chapter 14.

WHY USE AN INDEX?

Even though in some reference works, such as encyclopedias or directories, the entries are arranged in alphabetical order, there is also an index. You may ask, why would you bother to use it? The following situations demonstrate why an index can be important:

Your topic may be covered in a reference work, but not under the heading you expect. The term you have in mind may appear as an access term in the index, thus guiding you to the right heading in the list of entries.

Topic: Uses of seaweed
Entry in list under the heading "Seaweed": None
Entry in index: Seaweed. See Algae, marine p. 32
Relevant entry in list: Algae, marine.

There may be no single entry on your topic, but useful information may be scattered throughout other entries. Unless you use the index, you would miss the information altogether.

Topic: Drug addiction
Entry in list under the headings "Drug addiction" and
"Addiction, drug": None
Entry in index: Drug addiction
        Heroin addiction, 781–3
        Substance abuse, 1768–74
Relevant entries in list: Heroin addiction, Substance abuse.

Finally, even though there may be an entry for your topic under the heading you expected, not all the information on the topic may be presented there. By failing to use the index, you would miss additional information that might be useful in your search.

Topic: Using film and video in teaching
Entry in list under the heading: Film in education
Entry in index: Film in education, 406–29
       audiovisual instruction, 95–96
       curriculum (applications of film
        to), 337–39
       instructional film (as influenced by
        commercial), 621
Other relevant entries in list: Audiovisual instruction; Curriculum; Instructional film.

ELECTRONIC REFERENCE WORKS

Many electronic reference works were developed from their printed counterparts. Some are still available in both forms, while others are now available only on disk, CD-ROM, or online. Most are set up as *databases*, with information held in a structured form for searching.

In electronic reference works, the number and types of lists of entries, the order of arrangement, and the data elements may not be important to users. How information is held internally on a CD-ROM or in a computer database doesn't matter, so long as it is accessible. With respect to access, there are four types common to electronic searching, often with slight variations in how they are presented on screen. These are:

- browse access
- menu-driven access
- keyword access
- hyperlinked access.

Ironically, because computers offer faster and more flexible types of searching, publishers may not put as much effort into ensuring that information in electronic reference works is as well prepared for retrieval as in printed reference works. They may not provide any "see" references, for example. This means that even when an electronic reference work contains relevant information, if your access term is not used, the search will be unsuccessful. It is up to you to think of alternative access terms and try again.

The first three types of access are often used for searching library catalogs (see Chapter 15) and electronic finding aids (Chapter 19). The last is commonly used for searching CD-ROM encyclopedias (Chapter 5) and the Internet (Chapter 21).

Browse Access

Some lists of entry headings appear in alphabetical or numerical order on screen. To reach the entry you want, you are asked to type in the heading, sometimes called a *search term*. You may be taken directly to the heading once you complete it and press the enter or return key; or alternatively, as you type each letter, the list may automatically "fast forward" on the screen. You can reach the heading by typing it in full or by scrolling to it using a down arrow key.

The heading you select appears on the screen highlighted, flashing, or tagged by a symbol such as an asterisk. To view the information attached to the heading, press the enter or return key. Alternatively, headings may be numbered, in which case you enter the relevant number.

Menu-driven Access

Some electronic reference works provide a simple variation on access to alphabetical or numerical lists of entries. Rather than scanning and turning pages as you would in a printed reference work, you are given a series of menus or options from which to make choices until you progressively reach the heading you are seeking. For example, on the first screen you may be able to choose from the options "A–D," "E–G," "H–L," and so on. Having selected "A–D," on the next screen you may be able to choose from amongst "Aardvark–Alligator," "Alpaca–Archerfish," "Argali–Bassett," and so on, until you reach the heading—in this case, the name of the animal—you are after.

Menus also provide access to entries using concepts rather than letters of the alphabet. For example, in a reference work that provides biographies of scientists, you may be led through a series of menus that allows you to select the sex of the scientist (male, female, either), their field of research (biology, chemistry, geology, . . .), and the century in which they lived (twentieth century, nineteenth century, eighteenth century, . . .). Depending on the concepts you select, your search may result in none, one, or several relevant headings.

Keyword Access

With keyword access, you are asked to type in a search term or terms and press the enter key. The terms may be combined using logical operators, such as AND, OR, and NOT (see Chapter 10). After a short pause (sometimes indicated on the screen by icons such as a clock or an egg timer, or messages such as "Searching" or "Please wait"), the computer indicates the *postings*, or number of occurrences of the terms. You can then display the entries that contain these terms, with the terms highlighted.

There is also a less sophisticated type of keyword access: After typing in the search term, you may be taken to the first occurrence of the term. You must repeat the search to move to the second and subsequent occurrences.

Hyperlinked Access

Hyperlinks, or hypertext, is a means of connecting information in a non-linear manner. You can jump from one idea to another, which closely resembles the way we think—by association.

Hyperlinks enable you to follow an information lead. Words that are underlined, in capital letters, or highlighted; graphics with a border; and specialized icons can all indicate links to more information. You simply click on the word or graphic with a mouse, or touch it if it appears on a touch-sensitive screen, to create your own unique pathway through the information source.

WHICH TYPE OF REFERENCE WORK?

We have looked at the essential features of all reference works, both printed and electronic, but different types have different characteristics and idiosyncrasies. Figure 2–2 shows how the type of reference query determines the type of reference work needed, and indicates the chapter which describes each type of reference work more fully.

Figure 2–2 Test for choosing the most appropriate type of reference work.

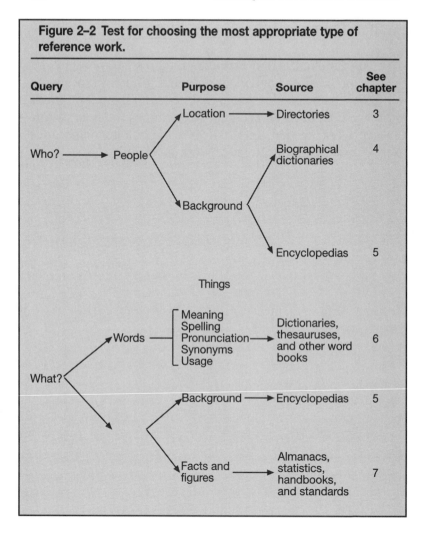

Query	Purpose	Source	See chapter
	Location → Directories		3
Who? → People		Biographical dictionaries	4
	Background		
		Encyclopedias	5
	Things		
What? Words	Meaning Spelling Pronunciation Synonyms Usage →	Dictionaries, thesauruses, and other word books	6
	Background → Encyclopedias		5
	Facts and figures →	Almanacs, statistics, handbooks, and standards	7

Figure 2–2 *Continued*

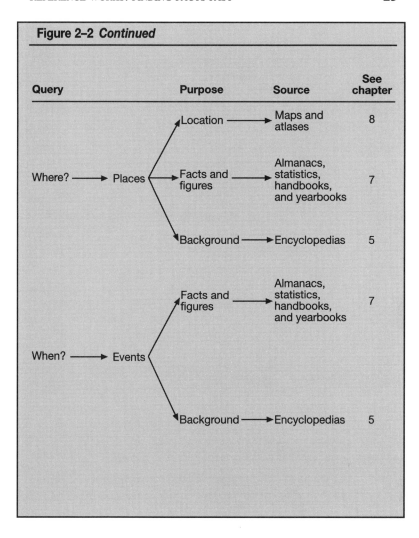

Query	Purpose	Source	See chapter
	Location	Maps and atlases	8
Where? → Places	Facts and figures	Almanacs, statistics, handbooks, and yearbooks	7
	Background	Encyclopedias	5
When? → Events	Facts and figures	Almanacs, statistics, handbooks, and yearbooks	7
	Background	Encyclopedias	5

3

Directories

Directories are most often used to identify and contact people or organizations, and in Chapter 11 you will learn why this is important. Directories are good for more than just "looking people up," however. Depending on the discipline you're studying, you'll find that they can be used in different ways. In marketing and public relations, directories can serve as special-purpose mailing lists for samples, direct advertising, or publicity releases. In sociology or demography, they can be analyzed to assess social trends or population dynamics. Across the social sciences, they can be used to select random samples for opinion surveys of products or political issues. And in history, obsolete directories can even be used to interpret the past.

CONTENT AND ARRANGEMENT

Entry headings in directories are usually the names of individuals or organizations. For individuals, data elements may include name and position; business organization and address; telephone, fax, and e-mail; home address and telephone; and religious, political, or recreational affiliations. For organizations, data elements may include full name as well as an acronym; address, telephone, fax, and e-mail of head and regional offices; brief descriptions of functions, products, or services; and names of important officers and their positions. Many directories are arranged alphabetically by entry heading. Some directories, however, group entries with similar characteristics: for example, geographic region, type of organization, product, or service. In this case, you may first need to use an alphabetical index if you are seeking a particular individual or organization.

TYPES OF DIRECTORIES

The one directory everyone knows is the local telephone directory. All the rules for using reference works apply here. You must be aware of the number and types of lists of entries, the headings used, and the order of arrangement.

In the *White Pages*, for example, government departments may be in separate lists of entries at the front. Alternatively, they may be in the main list of entries under a generic heading with a "see" reference from the first substantive word in their name to the entry heading (for example, "Health Department, Federal. See United States Government-Health and Human Services, Department of"). Other institutions, such as schools, libraries, and hospitals, may also be arranged alphabetically under these generic headings, or scattered throughout the directory under their own names.

Access to the *Yellow Pages* is alphabetical by products and services, and under each heading, alphabetical by company name. If you were looking for the Santa Fe Cafe in the *Yellow Pages*, you would first look for "Restaurants," and under this heading, for "Santa Fe Cafe."

There is also indirect access to the *Yellow Pages* through a comprehensive index. If you've gone on vacation and are looking in the *Yellow Pages* for the nearest place to buy a swimming suit but can't find them listed, try the index. It may have an entry such as "Swimwear. See Sportswear and swimwear—Retail."

There are numerous directories available on the Internet (see Chapter 21). *Telephone Directories on the Web* (teldir.com) provides links to these online directories from around the world, including *Yellow Pages*, *White Pages*, business directories, e-mail addresses, and fax listings.

Directories are also compiled for specialized groups of users, and some of these are listed in Figure 3–1. To give you an idea of the wide range of specialized directories, the following list includes a small selection of those located by browsing in just one library: directories of banks, silversmiths, geographers, railroads, campgrounds, post offices, historical societies, publishers, women lawyers, and stamp and coin dealers. Many are limited to particular states, regions, or cities.

To find contact details for U.S., regional, state, and local organizations, as well as international ones, try the *Encyclopedia of Associations*. Despite its title, it is a directory in three volumes. The *Congressional Directory* is the official directory to the United States Congress.

As a guide to the many directories available, *Directories in Print* lists contact and descriptive information for 16,000 publications worldwide, including professional, scientific, industrial, cultural, and other types of directories. Chapter 9 in this book will also help you identify directories in your own areas of interest.

USING DIRECTORIES

People move to different locations, associations change names, businesses get new telephone numbers, government departments amalgamate. Unfortunately, this means that directories are out-of-date in some details even before they are published.

Figure 3–1 Types of directories compiled for specialized groups of users.

Type	Coverage
Business	Manufacturers, retailers, distributors, and trade associations
Community	Local sporting, hobby, recreational, and ethnic social groups
Government	National, state, or local government departments and agencies
Institutional	Universities, museums, libraries, hospitals, foundations, and research centers
Media	Organizations and personnel involved in newspapers, radio, and television
Membership	Individuals belonging to political parties, religious groups, trade associations, clubs, and other organizations
Product	Generic and brand-name products
Professional	Individuals in professional associations, academic disciplines, working as consultants, or certified to practice
Social service	Medical, welfare, and housing, including those services specifically for women, young people, Native Americans, migrants, and people with disabilities
Tourism	Travel, attractions, accommodation, and restaurants

Some directories are published annually, and some even more often, to try to avoid this problem. For example, the *U.S. Government Manual*, which lists government departments and agencies, is updated annually, while the *Federal Staff Directory* is updated quarterly. For directories, then, it is important to note their frequency and use the most recent edition available.

Some directories cover the cost of publication through sales, while others are subsidized by association subscriptions and distributed free or at minimum charge to members. These are usually comprehensive and the information contained in them can be trusted. They may sometimes carry advertising to reduce publication costs.

Occasionally, local and regional business directories limit their coverage to firms that have agreed to pay for advertising space. They are often distributed free to increase their circulation. These should be used with caution.

Finally, it is handy to keep a copy of the telephone directory in your car. It is useful for finding alternative shops when the one you went to doesn't stock the item you want, for looking up the restaurant address you thought you knew but didn't, or for calling friends when you're running late. Think of it as the directory for handling minor crises!

4

Biographical Dictionaries

Directories will help you locate people, but you may also need to find information about people. For example, you may have heard someone famous giving a talk on campus and want to know more about their background. Perhaps you would like to find out about the CEO in a corporation where you are applying for a job, or about an author whose books you have enjoyed. Or you may wish to know about people's expertise and experience before you approach them on the telephone or at an interview (see Chapter 11).

Most often, however, you will need information about people to supplement your understanding of a topic you are researching for an essay or assignment. People often have a dynamic influence on the events of a period. As Thomas Carlyle wrote in his *Essays: On History*, "History is the essence of innumerable biographies."

For information about people, the type of reference work you will use most often is a biographical dictionary, sometimes called *collective biography*. You may also need to use a biographical index, but these are more complicated and are covered later in Chapter 17.

CONTENT AND ARRANGEMENT

Entries in biographical dictionaries are usually listed alphabetically by surname. Many sources also list nicknames, pseudonyms, stage names, parts of compound surnames, married names, maiden names, or full and real names as "see" references. Alternatively, the versions of the names not used as entry headings may be listed in a separate index. There may also be other indexes that are topical or that cover aspects of the subjects' lives, such as birthplace, year of birth, day and month of birth, educational institution attended, or occupation. Biographical dictionaries that specialize in longer, well-researched entries may also include indexes to the authors of the entries.

In a few biographical dictionaries, the lists of entries are arranged either geographically, chronologically, or by occupation. In this case, an index by surname is essential.

Entries in biographical dictionaries may vary from condensed outlines of facts using numerous abbreviations to full narrative or interpretative essays. The most common data elements in an entry are dates, titles, birthplace, family, education, qualifications, career, published works, religious affiliation, recreational or sporting memberships, and honors and awards. Useful data elements that may be included in some sources are pronunciation of names, portraits or photographs, bibliographies leading to more detailed information, and contact addresses. This last can be useful as a supplement to directories.

In a few biographical dictionaries that are updated regularly, the compilers save space by giving only brief accounts of those people included year after year, and refer users back to earlier editions for more detail.

TYPES OF BIOGRAPHICAL DICTIONARIES

There are many specialized types of biographical dictionaries, with possible coverage as indicated in Figure 4–1. When might you use them? Perhaps you are writing an essay and need background about a recent political leader, such as Margaret Thatcher, or a businessman, such as Lee Iacocca. The widest coverage of living people can be found in the group of publications called *Who's Who*. The first *Who's Who* was published in 1849, and contained a list of names of the titled and official classes in Britain. The present style of brief accounts, arranged alphabetically, was introduced in 1897.

Who's Who in America has been published since 1899. It is also arranged alphabetically, with a separate index volume that provides access to entries by geographic location, profession, recent retirees, and necrology (deaths).

Both the American and British versions have high standards of admission. They include people across a wide range of fields—politics and government, the armed forces, business and industry, the professions, and the arts—who are prominent or in official positions. As noted in its introduction (1997: vi), *"Who's Who in America* shall endeavor to list those individuals who are of current national reference interest and inquiry whether because of meritorious achievement or because of the positions they hold."

There are separate *Who's Who* volumes for geographic regions and women, and a few specialized ones based on ethnic origin and occupation. These include *Who's Who in American Jewry*, *Who's Who Among Black Americans*, and *Who's Who in the Theatre*.

For people who have died recently, check the latest edition published while they were still alive. Or try *Who Was Who in America*, which updates entries for people who have died and thus been deleted from current editions.

Who's Who or similar types of biographical dictionaries

Figure 4–1 Types of specialized biographical dictionaries.

Type	Coverage
Retrospective	Dead only, sometimes covering particular time periods
Contemporary	Living only
Universal or international	People from all countries, although they may be limited to international public figures rather than sports personalities or film stars. Some may include Biblical, mythological, or legendary figures
National or regional	People from a particular country, state, or region, who were born, educated, or made a career in that area
Occupation	People from particular occupations, professions, or subject disciplines, such as science and technology, law, medicine, art, music, sport, film and television, education, or librarianship. Authors are particularly well covered. Such specialized works have a long history, extending as far back as Diogenes Laertius' *Lives of Eminent Philosophers* of the third century A.D.
Gender	Both sexes, or men or women only
Fame	Notable and respected only, or popular and infamous as well

are also available for many other parts of the world, including Africa, Australia, Canada, China, and India.

But what if you are writing a paper for American history about someone long dead, such as Patrick Henry. In this case, you will need to choose a retrospective source covering the United States; the best-known is the *Dictionary of American Biography* (*DAB*). Or you might try *Who's Who in American History*, a historical volume covering 1607 to 1896.

If you're looking for someone who lived a bit later, say Henry Ford or Eleanor Roosevelt, the *National Cyclopaedia of American Biography*, which covers the years 1892 to 1965, is the most comprehensive American work. It is less limited and selective than the *DAB,* and has longer biographies than *Who's Who in America*.

Or, if your assignment is in English history, perhaps about the reign of Mary, Queen of Scots, the best retrospective source that covers Britain and Ireland is the *Dictionary of National Biography* (*DNB*).

If you are particularly interested in authors, you should also check the handbooks of literary criticism, which are described in Chapter 7.

Related areas that have recently enjoyed a growth in popularity are *genealogy* (the tracing of heraldic ancestry) and *family history*. If this is an area of interest, the best place to start is your local genealogical society. These societies often run "how to" courses, publish instructional guides for getting started, or recommend computer software for setting up family trees. Some research libraries now provide a range of resources to assist family historians, including materials on microfiche and CD-ROM.

USING BIOGRAPHICAL DICTIONARIES

It may prove important to know how the information in a biographical dictionary was obtained. Some sources rely on historians and other experts in the field to collect and validate information, often using primary or archival sources. Others, such as *Who's Who in America*, send entry data forms to prospective subjects. Entries in subsequent editions are updated by the subjects, who check and revise their earlier entries.

Where material is supplied by the biographical subject, there may be little if any editorial checking of content. Errors may creep in or facts may be omitted. The romantic novelist Barbara Cartland, for example, included her birthdate as July 9, 1904, in early *Who's Who*s, but then began omitting it as she hit middle age. The actor Walter Matthau indicated in *Current Biography* that his father, Melas Matuschanskayasky, had been a Catholic (Eastern Rite) priest in Czarist Russia who had run afoul of Orthodox authorities by preaching papal supremacy. He later admitted that he had provided this fake information as a defense against pompous and ludicrous questions. So remember, if you cannot find the information you want, or if what you find is questionable, check other biographical sources.

It may also prove important to know the authority of the publisher. Some publishers produce biographical dictionaries similar to "vanity" publications. They sell the work in advance of publication to the people to be included in it, and offer a range of leather-bound, gilt-edged options at exorbitant prices. People included in such volumes may only be those who are willing to pay.

Note, however, in the preface to *Who's Who* (1991: 6): "It cannot be stated too emphatically that inclusion in *Who's Who* has never at any time been a matter for payment or of obligation to purchase the volume." And similarly in *Who's Who in America* (1997: vi): "An indicated desire to be listed is not sufficient reason for inclusion."

As an aside, some of the more reputable publishers insert fictitious entries in their biographical dictionaries to discourage wholesale pirating of their material by other unscrupulous publishers. Should these fake entries be reprinted, a case can be made against the second publisher for infringement of copyright.

Finally, remember that there are other sources that can provide biographical backup, such as encyclopedias, dictionaries with separate biographical lists, and some almanacs. For people who have died this century, do not overlook newspaper obituaries if you can determine the approximate date of death.

5

Encyclopedias

Encyclopedias supply quick, factual answers to "Who?," "What?," "Where?," and "When?" reference queries. They are also a good starting point for answering research queries.

If you are working on an essay or major assignment, use an encyclopedia as a shortcut to gather background information. An encyclopedia entry provides a succinct outline or overview of a topic, including definitions and statistics; gives an explanation at an introductory level; and sometimes concludes with a bibliography listing books or journals for further reading. It will certainly not provide everything you need, but it will give you ideas for carrying out a more comprehensive search. For, said C.M. Francis: "Encyclopedias are the barebones of all subjects and the rotundity of none."

The word "encyclopedia" is derived from a Greek word thought by Renaissance scholars to mean the circle of human knowledge. Its actual usage by the Greeks and Romans meant a general education. The first work that can be called an encyclopedia was Pliny the Elder's *Historia Naturalis* completed in A.D. 77.

The Chinese were perhaps the most ambitious compilers of encyclopedias, creating almost 12,000 volumes between 1403 and 1425. The French *Encyclopédie*, prepared and published between 1751 and 1772 under the editor Denis Diderot, was censored, suppressed, suspended, and confiscated; Diderot and the printer were imprisoned at various stages. To learn more about the history of encyclopedias, look up the heading "Encyclopedia" in an encyclopedia!

TYPES OF ENCYCLOPEDIAS

You may already be familiar with some of the general encyclopedias. The *Encyclopaedia Britannica* is the most famous of English-language encyclopedias. A young Edinburgh printer, William Smellie, published the first edition between 1768 and 1771; the most recent printed edition is the 15th. It was claimed of this edition (Wolff, 1974: 37) that its pages placed side-by-side would stretch two-thirds of a mile, and that to read its 41 million words would take eight hours a day for a year. And a word of warning on spelling: *Britannica* has a single "t" (as in "Britain"), and a double "n" (as in "annual," "annex," or "annoy"—whichever you find easiest to remember!).

There are many general encyclopedias besides the *Britannica*, including the *Encyclopedia Americana*, *Grolier*, *World Book*, *Colliers*, and some important foreign-language encyclopedias. They all attempt to cover subjects across the disciplines of knowledge, but each has some special strengths. These are usually noted in each encyclopedia's introduction. Some are available in printed versions, some in CD-ROM, some online, and some in all three—although the various versions may not be identical in all respects.

Single-volume or desk encyclopedias cannot give the depth of coverage of the multi-volume sets, but they are useful when you need brief, factual answers—names, dates, places, and technical terms. The *Columbia Encyclopedia* is an excellent one-volume encyclopedia for quick reference.

Specialized encyclopedias concentrate on one discipline or field; they can therefore present articles in greater depth than general encyclopedias, which is extremely useful as an introduction to a topic. Some specialized encyclopedias cover broad disciplines such as science and technology, the social sciences, art, education, or library and information science. Others are much more specific, covering fields such as mythology, Islam, mountaineering, chamber music, or microscopy. Some examples include the *Encyclopedia Judaica* and the *Encyclopedia of American History.*

USING PRINTED ENCYCLOPEDIAS

The way an encyclopedia entry is set out may depend on the topic. For example, if the topic is a city, the entry may have seven data elements, with a set order of name as heading, followed by latitude, longitude, country or state in which located, date of founding, brief history, and important geographic features. If the topic is a person, the entry may consist of five data elements, with a set order of name as heading, followed by dates, nationality, profession, and brief biography.

Most printed encyclopedias are arranged alphabetically by topic, and can be accessed directly or through an index. The index may be in the first volume of a set, in the final volume, in a separate index volume, or in a separate series of volumes.

If the topic you are searching for is specific, then look directly for the heading in the list of entries. If the topic is broad or abstract (for instance, "energy" or "violence") and you do not know quite where to start, or if there are several synonymous terms that describe the topic, then look first in the index. Otherwise you may miss vital information.

In index entries, the locations usually refer to volume and page (for example, "Great Barrier Reef G: 325" or "Great Barrier Reef 13–216"), although a few also use a lowercase letter to indicate the position of the information on the page ("Great Barrier Reef, geological origins 12:390g"). You may need to refer to the introduction or explanatory notes in the index to interpret this letter.

USING ELECTRONIC ENCYCLOPEDIAS

The most comprehensive CD-ROM encyclopedia is the *Encyclopaedia Britannica*, which contains the equivalent of 32 printed volumes comprising 73,000 articles. The *Grolier Multimedia Encyclopedia* contains more than 33,000 articles from Grolier's *Academic American Encyclopedia*, and the *Microsoft Encarta* contains more than 42,000 articles and numerous special multimedia features. The *World Book Encyclopedia* is also available on CD-ROM, as are some specialized encyclopedias such as the *McGraw-Hill Encyclopedia of Science and Technology.*

Not only do these CD-ROMs provide printed text, but also pictures, maps, audio clips, video clips, and animations. For example, the *Encyclopaedia Britannica* contains 8,500 images, 1,200 interactive maps, and 30,000 related Internet links.

There are also a number of encyclopedias on the Internet. *Encyclopedia Britannica Online* at eb.com is subscription based, but much cheaper than the printed version. *Funk and Wagnalls Online Multimedia Encyclopedia* is at funkand wagnalls.com. Although use is free, you need to register with a password and be assigned a user name for subsequent visits. The *Concise Columbia Electronic Encyclopedia* is at encyclopedia.com and contains 14,000 short articles.

Searching electronic encyclopedias is far more flexible than searching their printed counterparts—and they won't get dusty on the shelves! The four basic types of access to electronic reference works (browse, menu-driven, keyword, and hyperlinked access—see Chapter 2) are all used in various forms in electronic encyclopedias, although they may be called more fanciful names such as "Category Browser" or "Find Wizard."

Let's look at some of these options using the *Grolier Multimedia Encyclopedia* on CD-ROM. Suppose you are writing a paper on pacifism as practiced by Martin Luther King, Jr. You could start with *browse access*, using a Title List search. This is an alphabetical list of the titles of all the articles. If you enter the terms "King, Martin Luther, Jr." or "Pacifism," you will find articles on these topics, just as you would if you had looked them up in a printed encyclopedia.

You could also browse the encyclopedia by Word Index, which lists alphabetically all the words in the whole encyclopedia, the number of times each occurs, and the articles in which they appear. For example, the word "Pacifism" is mentioned in 22 different articles and "Pacifist" in 41. Many of these articles are not related to Martin Luther King, Jr., however.

You could browse the encyclopedia as well by Timeline, which lists events chronologically from 40,000 B.C. to the present. When you select "1955: Martin Luther King, Jr., leads a boycott against racial segregation on buses," you are referred to articles on "Black Americans," "Civil rights," "Integration, racial," "King, Martin Luther, Jr.," and "Pacifism and nonviolent movements."

Alternatively, you could try *menu-driven access*, called the Knowledge Tree. Here you keep choosing options from a series of menus that become increasingly more specific. One pathway might be "History" → "United States" → "Social history" → "Civil rights." Another equally valid pathway might be "Society" → "Politics and government" → "Civil rights and liberties" → "Civil rights." At this point you will find several alternative menu headings that lead to the following relevant articles: "Civil rights," "King, Martin Luther, Jr.," "Pacifism and nonviolent movements," "Civil disobedience," "Pacifism and nonviolent movements," and "Black Americans."

You could also try *keyword access*, called Word Search, by entering the terms "Martin AND Luther AND King" (see Chapter 10 to find out more about the logical operators

AND, OR, and NOT). In this case, you will find 42 articles that mention his name, some of which ("Ballet," for example) will be irrelevant to your paper. More specifically, if you enter "Martin AND Luther AND King AND pacifism," you will be referred to three relevant articles: "Pacifism and nonviolent movements," "Civil rights," and "Civil disobedience."

Using Word Search, you can indicate that you want the terms to appear within the same article, the same paragraph, or within a set number of words. Similarly, you can indicate that you want to search article titles, article text, bibliographies, fact boxes, captions, or all of these.

Finally, you could use *hyperlinked access*. Within each article, the terms that are linked directly to other articles appear in uppercase letters. By clicking the mouse, you can move directly to these articles.

LIMITATIONS

A major limitation of all encyclopedias, even ones on CD-ROM or the Internet, is that they can never be completely up-to-date. As you can imagine, producing an encyclopedia is a mammoth task. Scholars who are specialists in their fields must be selected. Articles must be researched, written, verified, typeset, and proofread. Maps, tables, diagrams, and photographs must be prepared, and entries must be arranged and indexed. Printed and CD-ROM encyclopedias must be published, then distributed; and Internet encyclopedias must be formatted in HTML and loaded onto a server (see Chapter 21).

Obviously, there cannot be a completely revised, up-to-date edition of an encyclopedia every year, or even every few years. To try to overcome obsolescence, publishers use a policy of *continuous revision*, so that a selection of articles is constantly being revised and rewritten.

Publishers of printed encyclopedias also issue annual yearbooks to cover political events, sports records, scientific discoveries, and the like during the year. You should check yearbooks for events that have taken place after the encyclopedia's publication date or for the latest information on a topic. Note that the date of a yearbook is often the date of publication; the contents record events for the previous year. Publishers may also issue special supplements for geographical regions, such as Australasia.

6

Dictionaries, Thesauruses, and Other Word Books

In the seventeenth century, English was spoken by only a few million people in one corner of Britain. Today more than 400 million people around the world are native English speakers and more than 350 million have learned it as a second language. The English language is estimated to consist of approximately one million words (if you count obsolete, technical, and slang expressions) and most of them are recorded somewhere or other in a dictionary.

The word "dictionary" comes from the Latin "dictionarium," meaning word book; *lexicography* is the writing or compiling of dictionaries. Marcus Verrius Flaccus compiled the first general dictionary about 20 B.C. There are now many types of dictionaries, covering many subject areas, sometimes running into several volumes.

There are important differences between dictionaries and encyclopedias:

- The words listed as entry headings in a dictionary cover all parts of speech (the whole range of words used in speaking and writing), while the words listed as entry headings in an encyclopedia are all subjects (nouns).
- Dictionaries list each word separately, while encyclopedias may group information in larger chunks.

- Printed dictionaries arrange entries alphabetically. Printed encyclopedias also arrange entries alphabetically, but often have an index as well to guide users to specific aspects of a topic.
- Encyclopedias give information in more depth than dictionaries, particularly with respect to background knowledge.

CONTENT AND ARRANGEMENT OF PRINTED DICTIONARIES

Printed dictionaries and other word books are usually arranged alphabetically by entry heading. There may be guide words in the top margin of each column or page to indicate the first and last entries.

Although they may appear in different orders in different dictionaries, the data elements most often included in an entry are spelling, pronunciation (including sounds, and emphasis or stress), syllabication, capitalization, part(s) of speech, meaning(s) in order (for example, by history of usage or from most common to least common), quotations (showing examples of usage), word forms (including suffixes and irregular plurals), derivation or *etymology* (the history of the origin and development of a word), acceptability, and illustrations.

The style of most dictionary entries is set out so that the various data elements are obvious. For example, the heading may be printed in bold typeface; pronunciation, within parentheses; parts of speech, in italics; and derivation, within square brackets.

The view that the purpose of a dictionary is to set authoritative standards of word usage and acceptability is termed *prescriptive*. The view that dictionaries should record words as they are used, both properly and improperly—in effect, providing an inventory of the language—is termed *descrip-*

tive. Most dictionaries today record words as they are used, but label those considered non-standard or substandard as dialect, slang, colloquial, informal, taboo, derogatory, offensive, or illiterate.

DEVELOPMENT OF DICTIONARIES

Most likely you use an abridged dictionary. But such dictionaries are the by-products of extensive research into the history and development of word usage.

Dr. Samuel Johnson edited the first widely known English-language dictionary, which was published in London in 1755. Noah Webster compiled the first dictionary that distinguished American from British English in 1828. He also published a spelling book, known as the "blue-backed speller," that sold millions of copies and effectively standardized American spelling.

In 1879, Sir James Murray became the editor of the *Oxford English Dictionary* (*OED*), which was developed on historical principles. The *OED* showed the history of every word introduced into the language since 1150 and illustrated changes in meaning, spelling, pronunciation, and usage with relevant quotations. Murray finished about half of the multi-volume dictionary (A-D, H-K, O, P, and T) before his death in 1915; it was completed in 1928. The two-volume, photo-reduced compact edition was issued in 1971 with its own magnifying glass! The latest edition of Murray's monumental work, the *OED2*, comprises 20 volumes, defines over 500,000 words, and is supported by more than 2.4 million quotations.

Webster's Third New International Dictionary, published unabridged in 1961, was both attacked and defended for its permissiveness in recording current usage—in effect, changing from prescriptive to descriptive. Wilson Follett (1962: 73), for example, bemoaned the dictionary's " . . . dismaying assortment of the questionable, the perverse, the unworthy, and the downright outrageous," and asked, "To what is the definer contributing if not to subversion and decay?" Neil Lovett (1977: 18) noted wryly that, weighing more than 13 pounds and equivalent in volume to 14 cans of beer, it wasn't easily portable for the non-athletic student!

There are many other types of dictionaries and their uses today are wide-ranging. Depending on your purpose, choose one of those indicated in Figure 6–1.

USING DICTIONARIES

Although most dictionaries combine all types of words in one alphabetical sequence, some have separate lists of entries for certain categories of words or, in some cases, specifically exclude them. The categories of words that may receive special treatment include abbreviations, acronyms, foreign words and expressions in common usage, recent additions to the language, phrases, slang words and expressions, proprietary names or trademarks, genera and species, chemical compounds, personal names, proper nouns, names of countries, and geographic features.

Most dictionaries use separate headings for each word, but some save space by using a tilde (~) or other symbol to stand for an entry heading when it is used in derivative or compound words or phrases. Instead of being treated as separate entries, these derivatives are treated under the original entry heading. Thus, for example, "ant-eater" may appear as a secondary word under "ant," and not as a separate word appearing between "ante" and "ante-Bellambi."

Many dictionaries provide useful supplementary tables for quick reference. These may include Roman numerals, weights and measures, forms of address, mathematical tables, and Greek, Russian, German, Hebrew, or other alphabets.

Figure 6–1 Types of dictionaries and when to use them.

If you are looking up:	Then choose this type:	With these characteristics:
Day-to-day spellings, meanings, pronunciation	Abridged dictionary (known also as collegiate, desk, concise, or pocket)	100,000 to 200,000 entries (*Random House Webster's College* and the *American Heritage* dictionaries are recommended)
Unusual, archaic, or less common words	Unabridged dictionary	250,000 to 600,000 entries, often kept on a special stand (*Random House Dictionary of the American Language* is recommended)
Technical or specialized words	Subject dictionary	Defines terms used in specific fields, such as genetics or photography
	Glossary	Explains as well as defines terms in specific fields
Initials or abbreviations	Dictionary of acronyms and abbreviations	Covers initialisms generally or in specific fields
Changes in usage of words	Etymological dictionary	Traces meaning and spelling of words over time
Words based on people's names	Dictionary of eponyms	Examples of entries include "Braille," "pasteurize," and "bowdlerize"
Slang or regional English	Dictionary of slang or regional English	Contains words, phrases, and expressions; may be national or regional in scope (*Dictionary of American Regional English* includes colloquial speech in every part of the country; it is still in

Figure 6–1 *Continued*

Figure 6–1 *Continued*

If you are looking up:	Then choose this type:	With these characteristics:
		process. The *American Heritage Dictionary* is useful for American slang and contemporary usage)
Foreign words	Monolingual dictionary	Defines words using the foreign language itself
	Bilingual or translating dictionary	Gives word equivalents in two languages in both directions
	Polyglot dictionary	Provides equivalent meanings in three or more languages; arranged alphabetically by one language with indexes providing access via the others
	Lexicon	Covers words in ancient languages
Specific parts of things	Pictorial dictionary	Labels illustrations of equipment, plants, animals, and so on (Duden is a well-established publisher in the field)
Pronunciation	Pronouncing dictionary	Concentrates on proper names and difficult words; useful for radio and television news and interviewing
Rhyming words	Rhyming dictionary	Words grouped by accented syllables
Words to fit crossword puzzles	Crossword puzzle dictionary	Arranged by reverse or defining words, or by number of letters subarranged by positions of particular letters

Perhaps the best advice on using dictionaries comes from the early lexicographer, Dr Johnson: "Dictionaries are like watches; the worst is better than none, and the best cannot be expected to go quite true."

THESAURUSES

The word "thesaurus" comes from a Greek word meaning treasure or treasury. Thesauruses differ from dictionaries in that they supply a "treasury" of synonymous words or phrases, rather than explaining the meanings of words.

Peter Mark Roget, a physician and university professor, invented the thesaurus. Although earlier in his life he had made notes on a scheme for classifying groups of words rather than listing them alphabetically, he worked on the compilation in his retirement, beginning at the age of 61 and completing it 12 years later. His *Thesaurus of English Words and Phrases, Classified and Arranged so as to Facilitate the Expression of Ideas and Assist in Literary Composition* was published in 1852 and became an immediate success.

In the current edition of this work the words of the English language are initially grouped into named sections, each identified with a numerical code between 1 and 1,000 (for example, "959 Drunkenness"). Subsidiary order is numerical, with words of like part of speech (primarily noun, verb, adjective, and adverb) or other aspect appearing together (for example, within 959: "1. *n.* insobriety, intoxication, inebriation . . . 4. *n.* liquor, spirits, intoxicant, strong drink, grog . . . 15. *v.* tipple, nip, guzzle, quaff . . . ").

The need for a thesaurus in composition has not decreased, and numerous others have been published over the last century. When might you need one?

There are times when you may know what you want to say, but just cannot think of the appropriate word. By beginning with another word or phrase that is not the one you have in mind, but has some connection, you can use the thesaurus to lead you to the right word. Or you may be using one word repeatedly in an essay, and wish desperately that you could think of a different word to break the monotony. You can use the thesaurus to lead you from this overused word to alternatives.

In some thesauruses, the list of entries is arranged alphabetically, similarly to a dictionary. In others, the list follows Roget's traditional classified arrangement and requires a comprehensive index. You will need to go through the following steps to use thesauruses with classified arrangements:

1. Look up the word you have in mind in the index (located in the back section).
2. Choose the relevant aspect or meaning of the word from among those listed, and note the location—either the classification code followed by a period and a number, or the classification code followed by an abbreviation for a part of speech.
3. Look up the classification code in the front section, then search within that entry for the appropriate number or part of speech. Note that even though periods may precede the numbers, they are in sequence as if they were cardinal numbers and not decimal fractions—that is, the sequence is 1, 2, . . . , 10, 11, . . . and not .1, .11, .12, . . . , .2, ...
4. Note the synonyms listed with your word and choose the one that seems most appropriate. If the synonyms listed are not familiar, check their definitions in a dictionary before using them. Although they may be synonymous with the word you started with, they may have connotations that would make them inappropriate in the context in which you wish to use them.

USING ELECTRONIC DICTIONARIES AND THESAURUSES

Many of today's word-processing software packages include a built-in "dictionary" (in effect, a spelling, grammar, and hyphenation check) and thesaurus. How you use them depends on your software. In a Windows package, you can access these applications under "Tools" on the menu bar, whereas in other packages they may appear under "Library" applications.

The spell checker compares all the words in your essay or assignment with those in its database and queries any that it doesn't recognize. For any unidentified word, you can choose one from those displayed (they are the ones that most closely approximate the unidentified word) and replace it. Alternatively, if the unidentified word is a specialized one that you will be using regularly, you can add it to the database so that the computer no longer queries the spelling.

The thesaurus displays alternative words for the one you have highlighted; you may have to indicate the appropriate meaning and part of speech in order to narrow the choices. You have the option of replacing the highlighted word or retaining it.

Many dictionaries and thesauruses are available in electronic formats separately from word-processing software. For example, on the CD-ROM Deluxe Audio Edition of *Merriam-Webster's Collegiate Dictionary*, you can hear the authoritative oral pronunciation of more than 100,000 words, in addition to checking definitions and spelling. Or on the *OED2* CD-ROM you can search all 59 million words of text either conventionally or in new ways to reveal "hidden" information, such as the words with an Arabic derivation or the quotations from Jane Austen's works.

At Merriam-Webster Online (m-w.com/home.htm) you can consult the *WWWebster Dictionary* and *WWWebster Thesaurus*. A database of more than 17,000 acronyms, main-

tained from University College in Cork, Ireland, is at ucc.ie/ info/net/acronyms/acro.html. You can ask for help from other users if you can't find the acronym you want, or you can scan the list of unidentified acronyms to volunteer an answer.

To find other dictionaries and thesauruses on the Internet, consult *Yahoo!* at yahoo.com/Reference/ or *My Virtual Reference Desk Fastfacts* at refdesk.com/fastfact.html.

OTHER WORD BOOKS

Besides dictionaries and thesauruses, there are other useful word books for preparing assignments. Collections of quotations or proverbs are helpful, particularly when you are giving a class presentation and want to brighten it up with a pithy or clever introduction, focus, or conclusion. When searching for a particular quotation, it saves time to search in the index for the most distinctive or least common word first.

Books on the usage of words supplement dictionaries by analyzing and correcting faults in written English, and by discussing distinctions in the meanings of words and idioms. Style manuals, such as those listed in Chapter 14 Figure 14–2, provide guidelines for the presentation of text, footnotes, and bibliographies in essays and assignments, as well as journal articles. The *U.S. Government Style Manual* sets the presentation standard for government publications.

Concordances are alphabetical lists of the substantive words in a work as they occur in context. They are useful if you are studying literature and wish to know how often and in what context authors referred to particular topics. Concordances are available for the works of many famous authors such as Chaucer, Shakespeare, and Marlowe, as well as for religious works such as the Bible.

Compiling a concordance used to be a painstaking task. History has it that Alexander Cruden, who published a con-

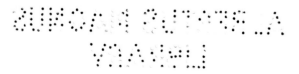

cordance to the King James Version of both the Old and New Testaments in 1737, was confined to and then escaped from a lunatic asylum after completing his work. Concordances are now produced with less trauma by computer and are available on CD-ROM. In this form, the full text of authors' works are searchable by individual words, phrases, or exact quotes.

Microsoft Bookshelf on CD-ROM comprises a dictionary, thesaurus, dictionary of quotations, almanac, chronology, concise encyclopedia, and maps; it bills itself as a multimedia reference library. You can search for an entry heading in a particular reference work using the "table of contents," or alternatively, you can search for an access term anywhere in the text of one or all of the reference works.

7

Almanacs, Statistics, Handbooks, and Standards

Almanacs, statistical yearbooks, news digests, census data, handbooks, manuals, catalogs, and standards are all reference works that contain miscellaneous facts. Each also has distinguishing characteristics.

ALMANACS

William Katz (1992: 286) has likened almanacs to encyclopedias "stripped of adjectives and adverbs and limited to a skeleton of information." They are usually issued annually and compress a wealth of facts and figures, both current and retrospective, into one volume.

Almanacs originated to supply calendar and astronomical data. The word was first used by Roger Bacon in the thirteenth century, and Benjamin Franklin was well known for compiling *Poor Richard's Almanack*. Among today's English-language almanacs, two go as far back as 1868: the *World Almanac and Book of Facts* published in the United States and Whitaker's *Almanac* published in Britain. *Information Please*, first published in 1947, is another frequently used American almanac.

Today there are almanacs and fact books from a variety of countries, including the *Canadian Almanac and Directory* and *Almanacco*, the annual book on Italy. Some states, such as Texas, also issue almanacs. A few Confederate states even published almanacs during the Civil War. Kane's *Famous First Facts* has information about hundreds of "firsts" in American history. For example, did you know that the first American passport was issued on July 8, 1796?

Almanacs have numerous lists of entries, with no particular convention as to the sequence in which they are presented. The contents vary, depending on publishers' decisions as to the scope (see Chapter 9) and the original source materials that were consulted.

Almanacs may include chronologies of the year's political events or summaries of trends in a range of fields, including art and culture, education, business and industry, science and technology, sports, and religion. They may carry lists of films, best-sellers, disasters, sporting records, biographies of important persons, obituaries, or crimes. Some give population statistics, brief histories, resources, and government administrations for countries of the world, or carry miscellaneous facts such as postal regulations, flags, income-tax information, and even crossword-puzzle guides.

Information is often condensed in lists or tables, and the better almanacs include citations to the original source materials. Some may also include longer, signed articles covering particularly newsworthy developments such as wars, elections, or scientific research.

In some almanacs the index is at the front, either doubling as a table of contents or located between the table of contents and the main lists of entries. In other almanacs it is more conventionally located at the back. The index may not include names of individuals, so you may have to look for them by subject. Finally, if you know the year in which an event occurred, you should use the almanac for that year and not the most current almanac to provide sufficient detail.

STATISTICAL YEARBOOKS AND NEWS DIGESTS

Statistical yearbooks are similar to almanacs, although they concentrate on statistical data and omit some of the miscellaneous information. The tables of statistics included often cover a time span, rather than just one year, which can be useful for making long-term comparisons.

Statistical yearbooks are generally arranged by country. For each they include basic information such as area and population, geographic features, government administration, and number of births, deaths, and marriages. They give facts on immigration, religion, education, finance, defense, communication, media, agriculture, and commerce, and they describe national symbols such as anthems, flags, and mottoes.

The *Statistical Abstract of the United States*, published since 1878, is the first print source for statistics of national importance, and provides ample references for additional information. *Historical Statistics of the United States, Colonial Times to 1957*, supplements the *Statistical Abstract* and includes comparative historical statistics.

Another very useful statistical yearbook is the *Statesman's Year-book*, which has appeared annually since 1864. Although published in the United Kingdom, it covers the world.

So if you are giving a talk on the growth in information technology, you may want to use the *Statistical Abstract of the United States* to include computer industry data on total employment in the field, hourly earnings, production, and the value of imports and exports. Or if you have a women's studies assignment to assess how closely the rate of population growth relates to the level of women's education in developing countries, you may want to use the *Statesman's Year-book* as your starting point.

On the Internet the *CIA World Factbook Search* (odci.gov/cia/publications/factbook/index.html) provides a variety of up-to-date information, including statistics and other data.

News digests are weekly or monthly loose-leaf summaries of news events, which are designed for chronological storage in binders. Indexes to the contents of the news summaries are included as part of the service; they are updated and cumulated at regular intervals. The best known are *Facts on File*, published in the United States since 1940, and *Keesing's Record of World Events*, published in the United Kingdom since 1931. Both are also available on CD-ROM. For greater depth of news coverage, see Chapter 17 on newspaper indexes and full-text databases.

CENSUS AND OTHER STATISTICAL DATA

The Census of Population and Housing is the largest statistical collection carried out by the United States Bureau of the Census. It is done every ten years. From the data gathered, the Bureau develops a wide range of products in many formats, including printed publications, computer disks, CD-ROMs, and microfiche.

The *General Population Characteristics* and *General Housing Characteristics* series provide detailed information on population and housing units, respectively. *Summary Population and Housing Characteristics* is a report series giving data for states, local governments, and American Indian and Alaskan Native areas. The *County and City Data Book* gives census figures for each county and most of the larger cities of the United States.

Summary Tapes Files provide census data on computer tapes. Users can select the type of census data (for example, age, education, housing, income, transportation, religion, ethnicity, or occupation) and geographic area (for example, collection districts, local government areas, zip codes, states, and protectorates), and view the results as computer-generated maps, graphs, or tables.

The Bureau also collects and publishes statistics on a wide

range of other activities—for example, industry, retailing, tourism, transportation, labor and unemployment, child care, families, and household expenditure. It supplies a core set of publications to 1,400 depository libraries so that they are readily available to the community. An additional 120 depository libraries receive the *Census Bureau Reports.* A statistical inquiry service is available via telephone. CENDATA, the Census Bureau's online information service, is offered through the information service companies Compuserve and Knight-Ridder (see Chapter 19).

HANDBOOKS AND MANUALS

Handbooks incorporate miscellaneous facts relevant to a particular discipline or subject, much of it presented in condensed forms such as equations, formulas, tables, graphs, or charts. Practitioners use them for quick reference in a variety of professions, including medicine, pharmacy, physics, chemistry, mathematics, law, psychology, engineering, and librarianship.

Although handbooks do not generally cater to the lay public, there are exceptions. The best-known is probably the *Guinness Book of Records.* The idea for the book came from Sir Hugh Beaver, the head of the Guinness Stout and Ale Company in Ireland, who wanted a book for bartenders to use to settle bets and arguments. It includes records for the tallest, longest, fastest, highest, smallest, shortest, and so on, across the range of natural phenomena and human (some might say inhuman, concerning records for oyster eating, apple peeling, and continuous roller skating) endeavor.

There are other useful exceptions. Of particular value to students are university handbooks. You have probably used yours to check on course requirements and class descriptions before enrolling. But they also provide information on staff, facilities and services, scholarships and prizes, tuition and financial assistance, committee structures, and university regulations; many include the university calendar and a campus map. Most university libraries and career centers maintain up-to-date collections for universities throughout the United States.

Also of interest are handbooks that describe various universities and their courses. These include *Lovejoy's Guide to Four-Year Colleges* and *Barron's Profiles of American Colleges*. The *College Blue Book* is a good place to seek information on college programs of interest. It will also give you information on financial assistance, foreign universities, accreditation standards, and much more.

You may want to use *Peterson's Annual Guide to Graduate Study* if and when you are ready to pursue an advanced degree. *Peterson's* six volumes cover graduate professional programs; humanities, arts, and social sciences; biological sciences; physical sciences, mathematics, and agricultural sciences; engineering and applied sciences; and business, education, health, information studies, languages, and social work.

There are also guides to schools offering specific types of programs, such as *Barron's Guide to Law Schools*. *World of Learning* is an indispensable source for worldwide information on colleges, schools of art and music, research institutions, museums, and galleries.

Among handbooks you may find interesting are those that deal with dates, anniversaries, and holidays. Would you like to know when to observe National Procrastination Week? If so, look in *Chase's Calendar of World Events*. Other handbooks cover occupations and vocational guidance, names and nicknames, trademarks, nutritional content of foods, and legal rights for women, homosexuals, and ethnic minorities. Field guides can help identify birds, flowers, reptiles, insects, shells, trees, and fungi. Guides for writers, artists, and songwriters list markets for publication and sale of creative works.

Literary handbooks are a boon if you are studying English literature. The *Dictionary of Literary Biography*, with nearly 200 volumes, is a major source for biographies of authors, summaries of works, identification of characters, criticism, and bibliographies. *Contemporary Authors* and *Contemporary Literary Criticism* are also sources for authors worldwide. *Contemporary Authors* names works in progress in addition to providing bio-bibliographies. *Masterplots* gives more detailed digests of novels. Also of interest are book review digests and indexes, which are covered in Chapter 17. Similar handbooks provide background information about plays and music.

Manuals give instructions, rules, or procedures for performing certain tasks. They tend to be equated with "how-to-do-it" books. Subjects include parliamentary procedure, secretarial practice, car and bicycle repair, home improvement, first aid, health and fitness, sports and games, gardening, and etiquette.

CATALOGS, TRADE LITERATURE, AND STANDARDS

Catalogs provide guides to current market prices based on sales or auctions; retention of earlier catalogs can show how values have appreciated or depreciated over time. Catalogs most often collected by libraries cover items such as artworks, postage stamps, coins, rare books, classic automobiles, and antiques.

Catalogs, brochures, and price lists of products, spare parts, and other supplies are collectively known as *trade literature*. This material is as varied as the companies that manufacture and distribute it; it is exceptionally difficult to keep up to date. Helpful in this regard is the *Thomas Register*, which lists contact information for suppliers of a wide range of products and services, contains company catalogs, and has a trademark and brand name index. It is also accessible on the Internet at thomasregister.com.

Standards are formalized procedures that apply in business, industry, trade, or related fields. They may take many forms, such as specifications for equipment, products, and materials; codes relating to design, practice, or installation; methods of analysis and testing; or definitions of terms or symbols. Standards are developed to ensure uniformity and reliability, and to simplify production and distribution.

The American National Standards Institute (ANSI) prepares and publishes U.S. standards and assigns each a unique identifying code. For example, they include procedures for good and bad tree trimming, emergency eye-wash equipment, and water supplies necessary for fighting fires. ANSI is now incorporating standards established by the International Standards Organization (ISO).

8

Maps and Atlases

Maps and atlases provide geographical information that can help you find your way around a modern city or write an essay about an ancient civilization. You can use them for locating places or confirming their existence.

Maps have a long history, dating back to the early Egyptians and Babylonians. As the foreword to the *Times Atlas of the World* (1992: viii) states: "If the definition of a map embraces any depiction of terrain features, whether traced in sand or scratched on stone or bone, then cartography must be reckoned among the most ancient communications, preceding any system of writing by countless millennia."

A survey of students at one university revealed that practically everyone on campus used the map collection at one time or another. You may not become a regular user, but it is good to know how to use maps and atlases.

CONTENT AND ARRANGEMENT

Maps are usually issued as single sheets that can be folded, rolled, or stored flat. Many come as parts of series covering geographical regions such as countries or continents. *Atlases* are collections of maps, usually combined with an index, that cover parts of a city, state, country, or the world.

The "lists" of entries in an atlas or map series are not lists, but individual maps.

The arrangement of maps within an atlas or map series is usually spatial (see Chapter 2). Let's use some specific examples to explain this concept.

In city atlases or street directories, such as those for the Pacific Northwest published by Thomas Bros. Maps, the region covered is divided into grids of equal size that are numbered sequentially. These grids, much enlarged, form the content of the atlas in the same sequence. Similar types of grids are used for most map series.

For world atlases, rectangles of various sizes are drawn around regions, with references to the pages or plates on which the enlarged maps of these regions appear. The grids or rectangles are often located on the end papers, inside the front or back covers. Occasionally arrangement can be alphabetical, say for maps of states, provinces, or countries.

Each map in an atlas is usually subdivided again in a grid pattern, often using letters or numbers for columns and rows as reference points. The index to the atlas, normally arranged alphabetically by place name, gives a page or plate reference with the letters and numbers of the grid, or the latitude and longitude, or both, for each geographical feature included on the map. This enables users to pinpoint locations.

Like dictionaries, many atlases have supplementary "lists." These may include glossaries of geographical terms, astronomical charts, insets of city plans, world time zones, population statistics, and tables of distance or time for air, rail, and highway routes.

TYPES OF MAPS AND ATLASES

The types of maps and atlases available are wide-ranging in their content and coverage. To choose the appropriate type for your purpose, use Figure 8–1.

Figure 8–1 Selecting appropriate types of maps or atlases for your purpose.	
If you need to look up:	**Then choose this type of map or atlas:**
Representations of natural and constructed surface features, such as mountains, rivers, cities, highways, and railroads	Topographic
National, state, or other political division boundaries	Political
Elements of the earth's crust	Geological
Boundaries of land ownership	Cadastral
Population, rainfall, vegetation, language groups, time zones, religious affiliation, and so on	Thematic
Exploration, settlement, and political and military control over time	Historical
Natural resources, agricultural or manufactured commodities, imports and exports, and transportation	Commercial or economic
Topography of the continental shelf	Bathymetric
Ocean-depth contours, port plans, lighthouses, and the like for navigation	Hydrographic
Actual surface features and structures	Aerial photographs. Use adjacent 'stereo pairs' for a three-dimensional effect
Surface features produced from remote sensing data	Digital
Earth's surface with accurate projections onto sphere	Globe

Also useful are *gazetteers*, defined as geographical dictionaries or finding lists. Entries in a gazetteer may include the official, standardized forms of spelling of place names as entry headings, with latitude, longitude, brief description, population (for countries and cities), and pronunciation as data elements. Variant place-name spellings may be used as "see" references.

USING MAPS AND ATLASES

To use maps correctly you need to understand several concepts: meridians of longitude, parallels of latitude, projection, scale, and relief. If these concepts are new, seek help from a reference librarian in interpreting the information you find. You may also want to check the introductory pages in an atlas or map series. They include explanations of publication dates, policies on revision and reprinting, types of relief or projections used, notes on naming of places, and keys to abbreviations.

Although many maps use distinctive English names, some use the language of the country (for example, Wien rather than Vienna). Whatever the treatment of place names on the maps themselves, a good atlas should include all their variant language forms in the index, either as index terms or "see" references.

PUBLISHERS

In 1807, President Thomas Jefferson commissioned the first official survey of the United States coast, acknowledging the government's responsibility for providing maps and charts. The agency now responsible is the United States Geological Survey (USGS), which produces topographic, geologic, and other thematic maps. USGS also produces aerial photographs and digital mapping data that can be used with geographic information systems software. A digital atlas of the United States will be available soon.

One of the many USGS publications is *Maps for America*, a well-illustrated volume listing, along with other information, the cartographic products available. The frontispiece shows topographic maps of Mt. St. Helens before and after the eruption—graphically illustrating its fall from 9,677 to 8,364 feet! More information about USGS products and services can be obtained by phoning 1–800–USA–MAPS or by viewing their Internet site at www.usgs.gov.

Several non-government publishers also have good reputations in cartography, and you can usually rely on the accuracy of their products. They include Rand McNally, Hammond Inc., and the National Geographic Society in the United States; and the Oxford University Press and Bartholomew in the United Kingdom.

Like encyclopedia publishers, many map publishers have policies of continuous revision—that is, individual maps are updated from time to time, and not necessarily all at once. Thus, not all maps in an atlas or map series are equally up-to-date, so be sure to check for copyright dates on individual maps if this is important for your purpose.

ELECTRONIC MAPS

There are now dozens of CD-ROMs containing maps with related statistical or travel information. Many have software applications that allow you to manipulate data before printing. Good mapping CD-ROMs are put out by Times Books, Microsoft Corporation, and DeLorme Mapping Company.

There is an electronic version of the *Times Atlas of the World* called the *Times Electronic World Map and Database*, published by Times Books of Cheltenham, England. The *Complete National Geographic*, available on 30 CD-ROM discs, includes every map, picture, and article from every edition of the *National Geographic* since its beginning in 1889.

Mapquest, a site that displays street-level maps for most of the major cities in North America, is on the Internet at mapquest.com. The site also provides directions and distances for driving between cities that you specify.

LOCATING MAPS AND ATLASES

If you want maps for backpacking or travel, look in the *Yellow Pages* under "Maps," or try outdoor equipment shops, news dealers, or bookstores. Some cities have stores that specialize in travel maps and guidebooks, and Mapquest sells maps online. Many CD-ROM map products are available through computer software stores or catalogs.

If you want to know the best libraries to use for maps, look in *A Guide to U.S. Map Resources*, by David A. Cobb, published by the Map and Geography Round Table of the American Library Association. This guide indicates the major collecting institutions and their holdings by state. *Map Collections in the United States and Canada* and the *World Directory of Map Collections* are also useful. Many map libraries have Internet sites that give information about their collections and provide links to other map-related sites (see Chapter 21).

A good atlas is a worthwhile investment for a home reference collection. When I was a student, I could never afford one, so I was very grateful to my husband for bringing the *Times Atlas of the World* with him as part of his dowry. For, said William Katz (1992: 410): "The *Times Atlas of the World* is the best single-volume atlas available."

9

Locating and Selecting Reference Works

The unstated assumption to this point has been that these various types of reference works were at your disposal—that you owned them or could find them easily in a library or on the Internet. But what happens if you do not know where to find the ones you need, or if instead of finding just a few, you are confronted with dozens? How do you go about choosing among them?

In libraries, reference works are often grouped together in a special reference section because they are used so often. For this reason, they are often *non-circulating*: you may consult them in the library, but you cannot borrow them.

To find the location of reference works that you know by name (such as *Who's Who in America*), search the library's catalog by title. To find the location of particular types of reference works, either browse the reference collection or search for them in the catalog by subject. Figure 9–1 shows the main locations for browsing and the best access terms to use when searching the catalog by subject. These terms are based on the ones used in headings from the Library of Congress, which most libraries have adopted as a standard. They are explained, along with techniques for searching the catalog, in Chapter 15.

Note that the access terms in Figure 9–1 are often used in combination: for example, "Sports—Dictionaries—Chinese," "Rock music—Australia—Directories," or "South

Figure 9–1 Locating reference works by Dewey Decimal Classification (DDC) or Library of Congress (LC) call numbers in reference collections, or by subject searches in catalogs with Library of Congress subject headings.

Reference works	Call numbers	Types of access terms	Examples
Directories	Depends on subject	Class of person	Architects— Directories
		Geographic location	Chicago— Directories
		Types of organizations	Hospitals— Directories
Biographical dictionaries	920s (DDC) CTs (LC)	Dictionaries	Biography— Dictionaries
		Indexes	Biography—Indexes
Specialized biographical dictionaries	Depends on subject	Class of person	Journalists— Biography
		Geographic location	Japan—Biography
Encyclopedias	030s (DDC) AEs (LC)		Encyclopedias and dictionaries
Specialized encyclopedias	Depends on subject	Subject	Football— Encyclopedias
		Geographic area	Thailand— Dictionaries and encyclopedias

Figure 9–1 Continued

Reference works	Call numbers	Types of access terms	Examples
Dictionaries (English)	420s (DDC) PEs (LC)	Language	English language— Dictionaries
Specialized dictionaries	Depends on subject	Class of person	Artists— Dictionaries
		Subject	Botany— Dictionaries
		Geographic area or nationality	Dictionaries— France
Almanacs	030s (DDC) AYs (LC)	Nationality	Almanacs, Canadian
Handbooks	Depends on subject	Subject	Physics— Handbooks, manuals, etc.
		Geographic area	Pennsylvania— Handbooks, manuals, etc.
Statistics	314–319s (DDC)	Subject	Agriculture— Statistics
		Geographic area	Italy—Statistics
Standards	Depends on subject	Subject	Air quality— Standards
Maps	May be held separately because of format	Geographic area	Poland—Maps
Atlases	912s (DDC) Gs (LC)	Nationality	Atlases, Spanish

Asia—Population—Statistics." You may have to experiment a bit because, depending on the search software, entering the terms in different order may retrieve different information sources.

CHOOSING AMONG REFERENCE WORKS

Once you find the location of a particular type of reference work, say biographical dictionaries, what do you do if you are confronted by too many of them? The answer is to consult the most specific source possible based on what you already know about your reference query. If you want details about Toni Morrison's life, for example, you could try a contemporary American biographical dictionary—or better yet, one covering contemporary American women, African Americans, or American authors.

If you are interested in someone less famous—me, for example—you might try to piece together what you know. In the preface to this book, it says that I was in librarianship in Australia and wrote the first ediion of this book there. So you'd be right if you guessed that you could find me in a biographical dictionary of Australian librarians or Australian writers.

PARAMETERS FOR SELECTION

Choosing the most specific reference work from among those of a particular type may sound intuitive. In fact, you can do it quite systematically by analyzing parameters—that is, the factors that describe and limit what each reference work covers. The twelve most important parameters are described next, followed by the steps to take when choosing among them.

Geographical Coverage

Geographical coverage may refer either to geographic areas specified for inclusion, or to strengths or biases based on the place of publication. Specification for inclusion can occur at several levels: local (the Seattle telephone directory, for instance); regional (a guide to tourist facilities in the San Juan Islands); state (*Washington State Atlas and Data Book*); national (*Academic American Encyclopedia*); or international (*Times Atlas of the World*).

Sometimes coverage is international, but the place of publication may serve as an indication of particular strengths or biases. For example, the *Webster's New World Dictionary* (College edition), the *Concise Oxford Dictionary of Current English,* and the *Macquarie Dictionary* are all abridged dictionaries of the English language; however, emphasis is on American, British, and Australian usage, respectively.

Language

The choice of language will normally be English. There may be occasions, however, when you will need to use other languages. For example, when reading Rudolfo Anaya's *Bless Me Ultima*, the well-known Chicano novel, you may need to use a Spanish-English dictionary.

Sometimes there are advantages in using non-English language sources, even when English sources are available. Certain foreign-language encyclopedias have strengths in particular fields—Italian in the fine arts, for example. If you are primarily seeking illustrations or reproductions of art works, language need not be a consideration.

Dates of Coverage

The dates of coverage may refer either to time periods selected for inclusion or to the year of publication. Time periods selected for inclusion are not always clear-cut, particularly when people's lives or events such as wars fall both inside and outside the period.

The year of publication is very important for current information. Names of countries change with independence; people die; volcanoes erupt and change their elevations. Because of the time required for editing and printing, information may not be current to the date of publication, but only up until one or two years earlier. Sometimes maps or tables included in a source are older still. A reprint of an earlier edition will only be current to the original year of publication of that edition, not to the year of the reprint.

Sometimes you must consider both the inclusive time period and the date of publication. The choice of people included in biographical dictionaries is likely to reflect prevailing opinion, and figures thought important in their time may not be important from a historical perspective. Not until the 1970s have many women been considered worthy of inclusion in biographical works. Leaders of revolutionary movements may never be incorporated unless they ultimately assume power.

Discipline or Profession

Most disciplines or professions have a full range of reference works applying specifically to them. In the field of computing, for example, there are dictionaries of computing terms, encyclopedias of computer science, directories of computer professionals and computer equipment firms, handbooks and manuals of computer programming languages, and even "atlases" of institutions and their computer installations.

Discipline-specific or profession-specific reference works in almost all cases provide greater depth of information on a topic than do more general sources. On the other hand, the vocabulary used is often more technical, as the entries are written for specialists rather than the public.

Scope

Scope indicates the characteristics and range of subject matter, including limitations, that determine which entries are incorporated into a reference work. The scope may include those parameters already discussed, as well as characteristics distinctive for a particular type of reference work.

The scope of a biographical dictionary, for example, would determine whether the following types of entries were included: only the living, only the dead, or both; only females, only males, or both; and only the notable and respected, or the popular and infamous as well.

Inclusiveness

Inclusiveness indicates, within the scope specified for a reference work, the proportion of items selected for incorporation. Thus, for a dictionary, a rough measure of inclusiveness is whether the dictionary is abridged or unabridged.

Comprehensiveness

Comprehensiveness indicates the amount of detail, or number and type of data elements, included for each entry. Unless you are aware of the comprehensiveness of entries, you may waste time using sources in which certain data elements are not included. For example, some dictionaries include syllabication while others don't, and some biographical dictionaries include people's current addresses while others don't.

Authority

Authority indicates the reputation for quality and the professional acceptance of the reference work. It is based on the knowledge and credibility of the authors, editors, and publishers, as well as on the reliability of the original sources from which the information is taken.

You can best determine the authority of a reference work by reading reviews written by librarians or experts in the field. A quick test, however, is to look up a topic you know quite a bit about—for example, a person whose biography you have just read, the place you live, or a sport you play. If entries are accurate for people, places, or things you know, they are likely to be accurate for others you do not. If, however, they are inaccurate—take care.

Audience

Audience refers to the group of users for whom the reference work is intended, and indirectly, to the comprehension level of these users. For example, some encyclopedias are aimed primarily at children; others, at high school students; others, at adults; and still others, at specialists in a field.

Treatment

Treatment indicates the way information in a reference work is presented: Is it objective? Is it balanced? What is the style of presentation? For example, an English style guide may be based on extensive research into the spoken and written language, decisions made by a government committee, rules of thumb set down by a publisher, or an individual's opinion. In each case, the treatment of the information will reflect its origins.

Relation to Similar Works

Is a reference work unique? Or is it a revised edition of an older work? If so, what additions and changes have been made? Just because a more recent edition of a work is available, it may not always be the best one to use. For example, even after the arrival of the 15th edition of the *Encyclo-*

paedia Britannica, librarians were urged to hold on to their 11th and 14th editions because their treatment of some subjects was considered superior.

How do printed and electronic versions of the same work differ? Sometimes libraries acquire the same reference work in two different forms because they serve different purposes. For example, libraries may subscribe to weekly looseleaf news summaries for current awareness, but discard them after a year and keep only the CD-ROM version for research.

Format

Format refers to the physical features of the source, including the size of the print and the quality of the paper; whether or not there are illustrations, black-and-white photographs, or color reproductions; whether the typeface is typeset or computer-produced; and whether the work is looseleaf or bound. These features could be important if, for example, you want to make a photocopy or enlarge some part for an overhead transparency.

Format is also very important for electronic information sources. Information may be on floppy disk, hard disk, CD-ROM, or online. It may run on IBM-compatible or Apple-compatible computers, or both. It may have particular system requirements, such as minimum hard disk storage, designated operating systems, and sound or color cards.

APPLYING THE PARAMETERS

To decide which reference work is the most likely to answer your query at the first go, take the following steps:

1. Based on your purpose and what you already know about your reference query, define as many of the parameters as possible for the particular type of reference work needed to answer it.

2. Apply these parameters to the reference works available, based on the following important indicators:

Title, located on the spine, cover, or title page (the latter may include a descriptive subtitle) for printed reference works; and on the face or slip cover (of a disk or CD-ROM), an introductory screen, an accompanying manual, or other packaging for electronic reference works.

Date of publication, located on the *recto* (front) or *verso* (back) of the title page for printed reference works; and similarly to the title for electronic reference works.

Table of contents, which usually follows the title page for printed reference works; and is located in the accompanying manual or on toolbars or pull-down menu bars for electronic reference works.

Preface, acknowledgments, and introduction, which usually follow the table of contents and are often paginated with Roman numerals for printed reference works; and are located in the accompanying manual or on help screens, often accessed from a menu bar or by entering "?," for electronic reference works.

Immediately eliminate any reference works whose parameters would exclude an answer to your query.

3. Carry out your search, giving priority to those reference works whose parameters most closely match the parameters you have defined for your reference query. If unsuccessful, go on to those whose parameters are less closely matched.

In practice, this decision-making process may be more haphazard and instinctive than is outlined. You will start to take shortcuts by heading first to the reference works that look more comprehensive because they are larger, or by eliminating those that look old because you are after something recent. Nonetheless, the process remains the same, even though you have learned from experience to first use the reference sources that seem most appropriate.

A hypothetical example will show how this process works. Suppose you're reading a novel for English that mentions playing the hautbois. You have no idea what it is or how to say it. Because you're after the meaning and pronunciation of a word, you decide that the type of reference work required is a dictionary, and you carry out the three steps:

1. Apply the twelve parameters to your reference query. Although the word looks French, it appears in an English novel and sounds a bit old-fashioned. From the context of the novel, it seems more likely to be a musical instrument than a piece of sporting equipment.
2. Start applying these parameters to the dictionaries available. Since the term is used in English, it may be in an abridged dictionary or one of the dictionaries on the Internet. If not, you could try an unabridged dictionary or the *Oxford English Dictionary*, which contains archaic words and derivations. If you're still not successful, you could try a dictionary of musical terms such as *Grove's Dictionary of Music and Musicians*, or since it looks French, a French-English dictionary.
3. You may find it easily, depending on which dictionary you use. It is included in some, but not all, abridged dictionaries, and it is also online in the Merriam-Webster *WWWebster Dictionary* (see Chapter 6). It's pronounced "oh boy," not "howt bwoz"; it's from the Middle French meaning "high wood"; a variant spelling is hautboy; and it's an oboe!

INTERPRETING ENTRIES

If you have trouble understanding or interpreting an entry in a printed reference work, turn to the introductory section.

Usually located here are aids to using the work, including a key to entries, a list of abbreviations, the symbols used for pronunciation, descriptions of page layouts, and other explanations about the lists of entries or indexes. For an electronic reference work, consult the users' manual or help screens.

It is also wise to double-check the information you have found against what you already know about your topic. Many people have the same names; the person you find may not be the person you are looking for. The same applies to geographic features. And some words or phrases have quite different meanings or connotations in different countries. Take care.

Finally, do not panic if you use more than one reference work and find conflicting information. This happens for a number of reasons. In biographical dictionaries, for example, people supplying material may inadvertently, or intentionally, give incorrect information; or occupations, titles, or dates may differ because biographers have had access to different primary or secondary sources. In encyclopedias, foreign names or places may be translated differently. Dates may differ for historical topics because different calendar systems were used to calculate them.

And then there are clerical errors, bound to creep in during the compilation of any major reference work. Take me as an example. The directory, *Australian Library and Information Professionals*, misspells my middle name (it should be Diane, not Dianne) and has me graduating from a rival university (it should be UCLA, not USCLA).

Even the most modern sources are not immune. For example, early editions of the Microsoft *Encarta* CD-ROM encyclopedia carried a picture of the old Parliament House in Canberra, Australia, built in 1927, with a caption indicating that it was the new Parliament House built in 1988.

When in doubt, ask a reference librarian or a professor for help in judging the authority of the conflicting sources or for leads to more detailed sources that may explain the discrepancies.

IDENTIFYING AND LOCATING ADDITIONAL REFERENCE WORKS

If you have not been able to find the type of reference work you want, perhaps it's not cataloged under the heading or placed on the shelf where you expect it. In this case, you should check with the reference librarian or use one of the guides in Figure 9–2, which list and describe reference works.

New editions of these guides appear irregularly. Their authors and editors tend to change more often than their titles, so it may be best to look for them in the library catalog by title. Use the table of contents or index in the guide to search for the particular type of reference work you need. When you find one that seems suitable, look for it in the catalog by author or title. If it's not listed, check with a reference librarian, who may be able to direct you to another local library that holds it (see Chapter 20).

In the next chapters, we will be looking at the ways to answer research queries, using not just reference works, but also individual information sources in a variety of information packages located in a range of collections. You will find, nonetheless, that the parameters we have discussed are still applicable.

Figure 9–2 General guides to reference works.

Balay, Robert, ed. 1996. *Guide to Reference Books*. 11th ed. Chicago: American Library Association.

Bopp, Richard E. and Linda C. Smith. 1995. *Reference and Information Services: An Introduction*. 2nd ed. Englewood, Colorado: Libraries Unlimited.

Diaz, Karen R., ed. 1997. *Reference Sources on the Internet: Off the Shelf and onto the Web*. Binghamton, New York: Haworth Press.

Katz, William A. 1996. *Introduction to Reference Work: Vol. I, Basic Information Sources*. 7th ed. New York: McGraw-Hill.

Lea, Peter W. and Alan Day. 1996. *The Reference Sources Handbook*. 4th ed. London: Library Association Publishing.

March, Andrew L., ed. 1996. *Recommended Reference Books in Paperback*. 2nd ed. Englewood, Colorado: Libraries Unlimited.

Sader, Marion, ed. 1994. *The Reader's Adviser*. 14th ed. New Providence, New Jersey: Bowker.

Walford's Guide to Reference Material. 1996–98. 7th ed. 3 vols. London: Library Association Publishing.

Wynar, Bohdan S., ed. 1998. *American Reference Books Annual*. Englewood, Colorado: Libraries Unlimited. (Published annually)

Wynar, Bohdan S., ed. 1998. *Recommended Reference Books for Small and Medium-sized Libraries and Media Centers*. Englewood, Colorado: Libraries Unlimited. (Published annually)

10

Search Strategies for Research Queries

Research queries ask "Why?" or "How?" and require more complex answers than reference queries. Although some types of reference works will provide good starting points, you will usually need to synthesize information from several individual sources contained in a variety of packages located in one or more collections using a range of catalogs and finding aids.

To answer a research query satisfactorily, you will need to develop a search strategy or plan. Why bother? Because a search strategy:

- ensures that you seek the exact type and amount of information you need, not a lot that is extraneous
- anticipates which search terms are best to use
- suggests the best collections and finding aids to use
- approaches the task methodically rather than haphazardly
- makes optimum use of the time you have available to devote to the search

A general model of the steps for developing a search strategy is set out in Figure 10–1, and the chapter that explains each step in greater detail is indicated. Notice that the steps are iterative—they seem to go around and around, back to various collections, catalogs, and finding aids. Think of this

Figure 10–1 Steps in formulating a search strategy. Chapters providing explanations of each step are indicated in parentheses.

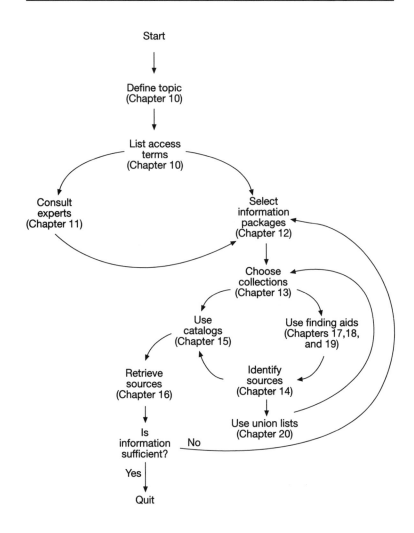

process as an expanding spiral: you are repeating steps, but in a widening arc to bring in more and more information sources relevant to your query. Let's look at these steps in detail.

DEFINING THE TOPIC

Most research queries consist of not just one concept, but the combination of several. It often helps if you can define your topic graphically to determine what is relevant and what is irrelevant for your information search. The best way to do this is to use logical operators and Venn diagrams. We'll first explain how this works, and then go through several examples to make it clear.

To use *logical operators*, you must first separate your research topic into its component concepts. For each concept, consider all the sources that contain information about that concept as being in the set (depicted as an enclosed area such as a circle), and all the sources that do not contain information about that concept as not being in the set (existing outside the enclosed area).

Use the logical operators AND, OR, and NOT (illustrated in Figure 10–2) to combine these sets to define your research topic. A bonus is that these operators will also be valuable for undertaking CD-ROM and online searches (see Chapter 19).

By the way, the process of using logical operators is also called *Boolean algebra* after the English mathematician, George Boole, who devised this system of symbolic logic. And the overlapping circles that show these combined sets are called *Venn diagrams* after the English logician, John Venn.

Figure 10–2 The descriptions and uses of logical operators in defining research topics.

Operation	Description	Use
AND	The occurrence of two (or more) concepts, where both (or all) are present	To limit a topic to componet concepts

A AND B

OR	The occurrence of the concept, or a second (or more) concepts, or both (or all)	To expand a concept to include synomyms or closely related terms.

A OR B

NOT	The exclusion of one part of a concept as represented by another concept	To narrow a topic by excluding tangenial or extraneous concepts related to it; or to narrow a search by aspects other than its component concepts, for example, by date or language

A NOT B

USING LOGICAL OPERATORS

Now let's go through some examples to illustrate this process. Suppose you are writing an essay on book censorship. Your research topic is not just about books, nor about censorship, but about the way they interrelate.

One circle would represent all the sources ever written or produced about any aspect of books (including their historical development, printing, binding, and publishing), while a second circle would represent all the sources about censorship (including censorship of a wide variety of art forms under various political regimes throughout history). The sources that are about both concepts would occur only in that area where the two circles overlap. You can express this topic as "Books AND Censorship," which is equivalent to the "A AND B" diagram in Figure 10–2.

Perhaps you feel that the topic of book censorship is too narrow. You decide to broaden the topic to include films— that is, either "Books" as a concept, or "Films" as a concept, or both—expressed as "Books OR Films." This is equivalent to the "A OR B" diagram in Figure 10–2.

You can then combine these two OR-operated concepts with the concept "Censorship", expressed as "(Books OR Films) AND Censorship" and illustrated in Figure 10–3a.

Alternatively you may wish to narrow your topic, concentrating on books without sexual content. This can be expressed as "Books NOT Sex," which is equivalent to the "A NOT B" diagram in Figure 10–2.

The AND operator can be combined with the NOT operator to express the revised topic of censorship of books for reasons other than their sexual content—that is, as "(Books AND Censorship) NOT Sex." This is shown in Figure 10–3b. Alternatively, you could narrow your topic by discussing censorship of political books. This can be expressed as "Books AND Censorship AND Politics," as shown in Figure 10–3c.

Figure 10-3 Examples of the use of AND, OR, and NOT operators to define a research topic.

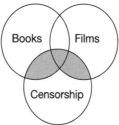

a. OR operation on two concepts comprising related terms, with an AND operation on a third concept: "(Books OR Films) AND Censorship"

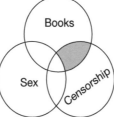

b. NOT operation to exclude a third concept from two concepts that have been AND operated: "(Books AND Censorship) NOT Sex"

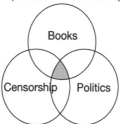

c. AND operation on three concepts. "Books AND Censorship AND Politics"

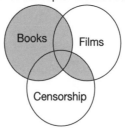

d. AND operation on two concepts, combined with an OR operation: "Books OR (Films AND Censorship)." Compare with example a, which shows the importance of sequence by using parentheses.

You must be careful to indicate the order in which logical operations are performed by enclosing within parentheses the concepts that must be combined first; otherwise, your results can be quite wrong. If, for example, the concepts in Figure 10–3a were combined as "Books OR (Films AND Censorship)," the results would be as shown in Figure 10–3d. In effect, you'd find information about the censorship of films, as well as everything ever written about *any* aspect of books—not just their censorship.

If you are not sure about some of the concepts in your topic (the way they are defined or what they cover, for instance), you can consult a reference work. To define a concept, use a general or specialized subject dictionary. To check dates or other facts, try an almanac or handbook. To determine a location, try an atlas. For an introduction to or overview of the topic or its component concepts, use a general or a specialized subject encyclopedia.

LISTING ACCESS TERMS

Once you have defined the topic, the next question is how to start looking for information about it. You may run into a number of difficulties here:

- Although there may be information sources that cover all the concepts in your research topic exactly, this is not always the case. You may need to use information sources that cover only one concept or a partial combination of concepts, and do the synthesizing yourself.
- Even if there are information sources that cover all the concepts in your research topic, the catalogs and finding aids listing these sources may not use all the concepts as part of the access term.

  In the example in Figure 10–3a, the access term used in a catalog may simply be "Censorship." You would need to go through the list of information sources under this heading and note those discussing books rather than plays, films, the Internet, or other media. Or in the example in Figure 10–3c, even if you find "Books— Censorship" as the access term in a finding aid, you would need to look at all the sources listed and choose only those that discuss censorship from a political rather than a sexual angle.

- Whether or not information sources cover all or just some of the concepts in your research topic, the catalogs and finding aids listing these sources may use terms different from yours. They may also use terms different from each other. These terms may be synonymous, broader, or narrower.

Figure 2–1 illustrated the types of relationships between access terms and entry headings. These relationships apply as much to catalogs and finding aids as they do to reference works. Before you start looking for information, then, you should make a list of possible access terms that describe each of the concepts in your research topic. You may need to expand the list, or alternatively, eliminate some of the terms, once you start searching and get a better feel for whether and how they are being used.

Let's apply this process to the example in Figure 10–3a. Possible synonymous terms are listed below:

Books	**Films**	**Censorship**
Publications	Motion pictures	Banning
	Movies	Suppression
	Cinema	

In addition, the term "Media" is a broader term that could include both books and films. You might also want to use a narrower subset of the term "Books," comprising some famous books that have been censored, to provide specific examples: say, *Catcher in the Rye, Lady Chatterley's Lover,* or *Tropic of Cancer.*

TERMS FOR STARTERS

Next you have to decide which of the concepts in your topic you will look for first. Why "Censorship" rather than "Books"? Or "Movies" rather than "Films"? The answer to this question is not always clear-cut, but there are a few rules of thumb:

- If your topic is fairly broad, start with the narrowest concept, the one by which the fewest information sources are likely to be listed. For the example in Figure 10–3a, you would choose "Censorship" rather than "Books" or "Films," because it is the narrowest.

  Use this term or its synonyms for searching library catalogs (see Chapter 15). This should lead you to relevant books on the shelves. Then use the index at the back of each book to look up specific examples or case studies to illustrate the generalizations you are making.
- If your topic is very narrow (for example, the political pressure on libraries to remove books about same sex couples, such as *Heather Has Two Mommies* by Leslea Newman and *Daddy's Roommate* by Michael Willhorte), you may need to think of a broader term to use as a starting point in the library catalog—in this case, probably "Censorship" again!
- Use more specific terms for searching both printed and electronic indexes and abstracting journals (see Chapters 17 and 19). This is because indexes concentrate on journal articles, which are likely to have a more specific focus than books.
- For indexes in a particular discipline, use the terms least common to that discipline. In the example in Figure 10–3c, use the terms "Books" or "Censorship" (or their synonyms) if you are searching political science indexes, but use the terms "Censorship" or "Politics" (or their synonyms) if you are searching librarianship indexes.

- For printed indexes, if an access term covers two or more concepts that pertain to your topic, use it in preference to a term that covers only one concept. Using this term will be more fruitful than using any of the terms individually, because a great many irrelevant sources will already have been excluded.

  In the example in Figure 10–3c, such a combined access term might be "Political Censorship." In this case you need only eliminate articles about political censorship of media other than books (such as films or newspapers) that are listed under the heading. Had you used just "Censorship," you would need to have eliminated articles about sexual and religious censorship of books, films, newspapers, and other media, as well as political censorship of films, newspapers, and other media.

As you become more adept at searching, you will gain a feeling for which terms are more likely to be used in which sources. Additional examples of searching techniques are also provided in later chapters.

11

Consulting the Experts

People are among the most important information sources for answering research as well as reference queries. People can give you information on the spot. They can explain things you don't understand, give you leads for further searching, and show you how to use different types of information packages effectively.

Begin by contacting a reference librarian at your college or university. Reference librarians can help you define the topic more clearly or determine the most appropriate search terms. During the search, they can suggest the most important information sources or the best collections. Before you're finished, they can talk over your findings to be sure you're on the right track. Remember, reference librarians are there to assist you.

You may also want to consult professors on campus with expertise in your topic or other knowledgeable people off-campus. The three essentials for getting information from these people are the ability to use a range of directories; access to telephone, fax, or e-mail; and polite assertiveness.

DIRECTORIES: THE STARTING POINT

If you already know someone likely to be able to help you with your research topic—a friend of the family or a

97

roommate's parent—you are in luck. The only directory you may require is the *White Pages*.

More usually, however, you will need to find a person who knows about the topic. One place to look is in directories of professional organizations, such as the National Traffic Safety Institute or the Office of Human Rights, to lead you to authorities in a field (see Chapter 3). Or you may want to ring the public affairs office of an appropriate corporation or government agency, as they often maintain lists of spokespersons.

Another place to look is the *Yellow Pages*, but remember that you have no way of knowing whether the people listed are reputable and reliable. However, some *Yellow Pages* searches can be fruitful. For example, I found people to interview by telephone for an article on hypnosis and smoking listed under "Hypnotherapy." A friend interested in amethysts called the listings under "Gemologists," went to the most promising-sounding jewelry shop, visited the owners' home to see films of their mining trips, corresponded with them while they were away, and ended up spending her vacation visiting and working with them.

Your library should have telephone directories for other nearby cities, and many are available on the Internet in case you need to go beyond local resources (see Chapter 3).

MAKING CONTACT

Once you find a name, address, and telephone number, you may think you are halfway there. You are not!

The first time you try, the telephone number may no longer be in use, the extension may ring with no answer, the receptionist may never have heard of the person, or the office may be closed when you visit. Do not give up. Check that your information is correct and try again.

At your next attempt, the expert may not be available. You may leave a message but your call may not be returned.

Keep on trying until you reach the expert. When you finally do, he or she may use any one of a number of ploys to avoid being bothered. You will need to continue to question, politely but tenaciously, until you get the information you need.

Given all these difficulties, why bother with people at all? Because the right person can be a gold mine. The important thing is to control your own search.

To save time, always match your introduction to the level and authority of the person you're dealing with. In most companies and institutions, your first contact will be with an answering machine or a receptionist. Do no more than ask for the person you want or the position they hold. The best approach with your next contact, often a secretary, is to give your name and institutional affiliation and ask if the expert is in.

THE TELEPHONE INTERVIEW

When you get the right person on the telephone, there are five things you need to establish:

- who you are
- where you are from
- what information you need
- what you plan to do with the information
- when you need the information.

You are only a disembodied voice coming over a wire. For all the expert knows, you could be a debt collector or an IRS agent. In a couple of sentences, you need to introduce yourself and give enough background to establish your credibility. You need to communicate that you are an interested, courteous, and friendly person; that you are seeking help; and that you believe the person you are talking to can help you. If you have been referred by someone, be sure and mention the relationship.

For example: "Hello. My name is Nancy Lane, and I am writing a paper on homelessness among unemployed youth. My professor, Linda McGill, said that you might be able to supply me with the department's statistics on the estimated number of homeless youth in the city." Once you have determined that the person has the statistics, you may need to adjust the time: "Rather than your mailing them out to me, may I come in this afternoon to pick them up?"

If the information you seek is extensive, you may want to use your initial contact to set up an appointment for a personal interview. For example: "Hello. My name is Nancy Lane. I'm a member of the Student Women's Group at the University of Washington, and we are preparing a proposal to set up evening childcare facilities on campus. We were referred to your office by the Women's Center. Would you be free to talk to a group of us about what we need to put into the proposal, and how we should set it out?"

THE PERSONAL INTERVIEW

The rule for interviewing is: "Be prepared!"

- Be prepared with background on the topic. Learn as much as possible in advance from your library or through the Internet. You need to know enough to know what you need to find out from the interview.
- Be prepared with background on the interviewee. Ask questions on topics in which he or she has expertise.
- Be prepared for note-taking. Sharpen pencils; carry extra pens; be sure there are enough empty pages in your notebook.
- Be prepared with equipment. Always ask whether the person minds being tape-recorded. Put new batteries in your recorder. Use a new tape. Test the machine before you arrive to see that it is recording. Record the date and the person's name and position at the beginning of the tape.

- Be prepared for getting there. Always give yourself at least 15 minutes more than you'll think you need, in order to find the right office and compose yourself.
- Be prepared for the interview. Draw up a list of questions in advance, whether or not it turns out that you need them. Start with an easy, ice-breaking question (for example, "How did you first get interested in becoming a journalist?"). Move from general background questions ("What sort of training did you have?") to more specific ones ("Which universities do you think are the best now for training as a journalist?"). Ask open-ended questions ("What do you like most about your work?"), rather than ones that can be answered "Yes" or "No" ("Do you like working as a journalist?").
- Be prepared during the interview. Try not to interrupt the interviewee's train of thought, but make sure you cover all the essentials. Ask for the spelling of names or meaning of terms that are unclear. Keep an eye on the tape and your watch so that you know when to turn the tape over. But mostly listen.
- Be prepared for the follow-up. Plan the interview at a time when you are free to transcribe your notes while they are still fresh. You may go expecting to tape-record, but not be given permission. You may forget to turn the tape over. Or you may find that, despite all your precautions, the equipment was faulty and all or part of the interview is missing. This is why you need the time immediately, when you can still remember what was said.
- Check back with the interviewee if there is anything that needs verification. Write a thank-you note expressing your appreciation, especially if the interviewee gave you a good deal of time or went to special lengths to accommodate you.

ELECTRONIC CONSULTING

Through discussion groups and electronic bulletin boards on the Internet, you can gain access to people around the world who share your interests. You can find discussion groups on almost any topic—for example, the Hubble Space Telescope, Nepalese culture, or the molecular biology and genetics of yeast—where you can ask questions and seek advice.

Many discussion group subscribers are well-informed and willing to help, although there are crackpots and leg-pullers as well. Unless you know the reputation and credibility of a discussion group participant, you may want to seek confirmation of any response that could be suspect. For advice on accessing discussion groups, see Chapter 21.

WORDS FROM THE WISE

Even when you ask a librarian for help in finding information sources, you are carrying out an interview (although librarians are taught that *they* are the ones doing the interviewing!). In this case, it is important that you indicate what you are after as specifically as possible. You may want to take advice from the journalists whose life's work is interviewing:

Ron Redmond is the world wire editor in the National and Foreign Department of the *Seattle Post-Intelligencer*. He also served as the chief spokesman for the United Nations High Commission for Refugees in Geneva from 1992 to 1996. He said: "Having worked on both ends of the telephone, it's obvious to me that an interviewer who can demonstrate a sound knowledge of the subject will usually earn the confidence and trust of the person being interviewed. This in turn can lead the interviewee to provide much more valuable background on the subject."

He continued: "In my work as a UN spokesman, I was

almost always impressed by the professionalism of journalists representing certain organizations, foremost among them the BBC. Their interview style was always courteous, well-informed, and to the point. They would ask tough questions, but they would do it in a courteous and professional way. They asked the right questions and were quick on their feet—able to detect inconsistencies because they knew their subject matter.

"Although many large organizations provide all sorts of printed hand-out material, there is often no substitute for direct contact with someone in the organization. A good organization makes it a point to hire spokespeople who make themselves available for interviews. These spokespeople have a wealth of inside knowledge that can really add to the various PR publications their organizations produce. Use the spokespeople in large organizations. If they can't answer your questions, they'll find someone who can. Avoid long, convoluted questions. Get to the point and let the person know your question."

Douglas Underwood, assistant professor in the School of Communications at the University of Washington, identified a number of advantages of the personal interview, either face-to-face or by telephone. He said: "Questions can be developed and answers probed in a dynamic context that allows the conversation to move in unanticipated but important directions. For face-to-face interviews, body language can be assessed and evaluated to help determine in what directions to move the questioning. Quotes from personal interviews can add liveliness and vitality to the sometimes dry recitations of academic and other written sources in the typical research article or dissertation.

"Interviews allow the research student to explore new avenues opened up by the written source documents and to ask questions that go beyond the written sources. Live interview subjects can often give the research student other good places to go for information. Live interviews with authors of academic research articles give the authors opportunities to expand, explain the nuances, and go into greater depth about the material in their articles."

Ed Bassett has served as editor of the *Statesman Journal* in Salem, Oregon, and as copy editor of the *Seattle Times* and *Los Angeles Times*. He focused on interviews conducted by reporters, but added that the same advice applies to all types of information-seeking interviews: "The news interview is designed to have the reporter and source exchange questions and answers to sharpen a salient point for the reader or viewer. Interviews are most effective when conducted face-to-face. It is important to note that interviews are normally scheduled to pull together story elements that contain some complexity.

"In those situations where the reporter knows and is trusted by the source, the depth of the interview can be enhanced. In those cases where the reporter must establish a rapport with the source immediately, his or her skill in interpersonal communications can be crucial. In the case of the feature interview, the dimensions that can be added to the story are designed to hold the reader or viewer's attention throughout the longer treatment.

"Reporters should work with the sources to achieve the most complete story possible. When a story requires multiple interviews, reporters should attempt to achieve balance and be fair and complete. They should prepare for the interview, create a relationship with the source, work at the same level of thought as the source, be a good listener, and watch the reactions of the source. These reactions can be revealing."

Jean Godden, *Seattle Times* columnist, stated: "Talking to people, asking them questions, and asking them pertinent follow-up questions is the most important thing a person can do to obtain information. Whether these interviews are face-to-face or on the telephone, they are a critical method to solicit information. It can be more important than finding information in print, as information obtained from individuals is often new and different information not available elsewhere. Whenever students call to interview me, that is exactly what I tell them."

12

Selecting Information Packages

To answer a research query, you need the contents—the information itself. You cannot, however, ignore the information package—the book, journal, video, CD-ROM, World Wide Web, or other "container" in which it comes (see Chapter 1).

Why? Because identification and location of the contents depends on the type of package—first, because different types of packages are held in different collections, and second, because different types of packages may require different types of searching techniques. To begin a search you must thus have in mind the types of information packages you are after.

There are several rules of thumb for selecting among various types of information packages:

- Search for the types of packages that best suit your ultimate purpose. If you are writing an essay on federal broadcasting policy, established practice would be to search for and cite scholarly works and journal articles. Documents and annual reports issued by relevant government agencies such as the Federal Communications Commission would also be appropriate. If you are preparing a presentation on the topic as well, you may want to supplement this material with an excerpt from a current affairs program on videotape or a short segment from a politician's speech on audiocassette.

- Search for the types of packages where the information content most closely matches your own level of understanding and that of your intended audience. Information content varies from the highly technical to the mass market.

  Take the relationship between smoking and heart disease. At one extreme, information aimed at the medical profession uses specialist terminology. The medium is primarily print (medical texts, research articles, and conference papers), or occasionally audio or visual (audiocassette lectures for continuing medical education and X-rays showing diseased hearts). At the other extreme, information intended for the public is in common, everyday language in readily accessible sources such as newspapers, magazines, and brochures. It is often in an audiovisual format (posters, television programs, and radio talks by health experts).

  There is little point in seeking information you can't understand. Unless you are a medical student, your essay on heart disease and smoking should probably rely on articles appearing in the popular press rather than in journals for medical specialists. You may, however, want to interview some public health professionals who are able to communicate at several levels. If they use specialized language in an interview, you can stop them and ask the meaning of a word.

- Search for the types of packages that reflect the currency of the information you need. Television news stations such as CNN tell what is happening now. Regularly scheduled radio and television news programs tell what has happened during the day. The morning newspaper covers the events that happened yesterday; news magazines, the previous week; popular magazines, the previous month.

  Scholarly journals often publish research results long

after the researcher has gone on to new and different projects. The time-lag between receipt and publication of an article, depending on the frequency of the journal, may range from two weeks to two years. Several years may have passed by the time a book has been written, edited, published, and distributed.

- Search for the types of packages that present information from an appropriate point of view. What is it like being on welfare? To develop first-hand understanding, you may want to interview people at a food bank or social service agency who are willing to describe their personal experiences. Occasionally, the local newspaper may carry a first-person article or a letter to the editor.

  Finding second-hand information about people on welfare is much easier. This is the material of human-interest newspaper and magazine feature articles and television documentaries. Sociological research studies and government reports also focus on these topics.

  Then there are those who criticize or review, who pass comment on the comments of others. The information packages they use are reviewing journals, television current affairs commentaries, newspaper editorials, or anthologies of literary criticism.

  Choose how far you wish to distance yourself from the original source. The first-hand interview can often serve as a case study, providing examples of the generalizations in second-hand reporting. Third-hand commentators often give an interpretation, an analysis, or rationale.

- Finally, use technology as required. If you can operate your own television set, cassette recorder, radio, and telephone, then you can learn to use other equipment in media resource centers or libraries just as easily. Ask for help in dealing with whatever equipment you need, be it digital camera or computer projector.

INFORMATION PACKAGES AND THEIR CHARACTERISTICS

You may be familiar with most of the types of information packages discussed so far. As a college student, however, you will need to become aware of an even wider range of packages than you may have used in the past.

Figure 12–1 (based on Table 3 in Landau et. al., 1982: 87) lists types of information packages categorized by the medium of communication, format, and unique identifying characteristics. In some cases, these packages can be further grouped into subsets based on distinctive stylistic or textual traits. Although Figure 12–1 includes most of the packages you are likely to use, it is by no means comprehensive.

The best way to learn about these information packages is to use them. See if those you have not tried before are available in your university library or media center. You must also learn to recognize these different packages from their bibliographic descriptions, if you are to use library catalogs and finding aids effectively. This process is discussed in Chapter 14. Ask for assistance if you need it!

SINGLE-ISSUE PRINT FORMATS

Monographs or books can be written by one author, or two or more joint authors. Some collected works may have different authors for each section, in which case an editor or compiler has responsibility for the work as a whole. Monographs may also be written by a corporate body such as an organization, agency, or government department, in which case it represents the collective view of that body.

Monographs are usually intended as "once-only" publications. Depending on their popularity, however, some may be reprinted as part of the same edition, or revised and updated as a new edition. As monographs are of major importance

Figure 12–1 Types of information packages, categorized by medium and format.

Medium	Format	Types of packages
Print on paper	Single-issue publication	Books or monographs
		Pamphlets or brochures
		Ephemera
		Sheet music or scores
	Serial publication	Journals, periodicals, or magazines
		Newspapers
	Unpublished material	Correspondence
		Manuscripts
		Archives or administrative records
Print on film	Microform	Microfilms
		Microfiche
		Computer output microforms (COM)
Print on disk	Electronic	Floppy disks
		Hard disks
		CD-ROMs
Print by transmission	Telecommunications network	Facsimile (fax)
	Computer network, including the Internet	Online retrieval
		FTP file transfer
		Electronic texts
Audio	Sound recording	Phonograph records
		Reel-to-reel tape recordings
		Audiocassettes
		Compact discs (CDs)
		Digital audiotape
	Broadcast	Radio

Figure 12–1 *Continued*

Figure 12–1 *Continued*

Medium	Format	Types of packages
Visual	Graphic	Drawings or illustrations
		Paintings
		Art prints or
		reproductions
		Posters
		Photographic prints
		Technical drawings
	Projected	Overhead transparencies
		35-mm transparencies or
		slides
		Holograms
	Electronic	Digital images
	Three-dimensional object	Realia or specimens
		Toys, games, or puzzles
		Samples
		Models
		Dioramas
	Cartographic	Maps or atlases
		Globes
Audiovisual (AV, non-print)	Video	Videocassettes or
		videotapes
		Videodiscs
	Projected	Films (motion pictures
		or movies)

in preparing essays and assignments, you should become familiar with the terminology applied to their specific parts, as set out in Appendix 2.

Some monographs have distinctive stylistic or textual traits. These include *anthologies* (collections of literary pieces of varied authorship), *conference proceedings* (printed

Figure 12–1 *Continued*		
Medium	**Format**	**Types of packages**
	Broadcast	Television
		Digital television (DTV)
		High definition television (HDTV)
Multimedia	Multiple formats	Kits
	Electronic	Multimedia CD-ROMs
		Compact disc interactive (CD-I)
		Digital versatile discs (DVD)
	Computer network, including the Internet	World Wide Web
Interpersonal	Individual personal contact	Interviews or consultations
	Group personal contact	Talks or lectures
		Seminars, conferences, or workshops
		Meetings
		Class discussions
	Telecommunications network	Telephone conversations
		Teleconferences
	Computer network	E-mail
		Electronic bulletin boards or discussion groups
		Electronic mailing lists

versions of papers presented at conferences or meetings of professional associations), *technical reports* (publications resulting from research or development work, often issued in a numbered sequence), *government documents* (publications issued by or on behalf of federal, state, and local governments), and *theses* or *dissertations* (research studies presented for postgraduate degrees, usually produced in limited numbers of copies).

Pamphlets are defined as works of about 50 pages or less, often stapled rather than bound. Those with particular characteristics include *trade literature* (equipment and supply catalogs) and *patents* (government grants protecting an exclusive right to the design and manufacture of an invention or discovery). *Ephemera* are materials of transitory value, often issued for particular occasions, such as theater tickets, music programs, and campaign materials. They may be stored on shelves in pamphlet boxes or in folders in filing cabinets, and are sometimes called *vertical file materials*. Not all libraries catalog these types of materials individually.

Printed music, including sheet music and scores, may be cataloged in several different ways, especially in conservatory collections: by the composer, title, style (for example, jazz, classical, or rock), level of difficulty, and number and types of voices or instruments.

SERIAL PRINT FORMATS

Serials are also known as periodicals, journals, and in their more popular form, magazines. They differ from monographs in that they are published at regular intervals and are intended to be continued indefinitely. Each volume (the first year starting as volume 1) comprises one year's accumulation, with a set number of issues to each volume.

The pages in each issue may be numbered starting with page 1; or they may be numbered starting with page 1 in the first issue, continuing sequentially through each issue, then starting again at page 1 in the next volume. Although a volume is usually equivalent to "a year's worth," it may not correspond to a calendar year, but run, say, from July of one year to June of the following year.

There are also hybrids among monograph and serial publications. Some monographs may be issued in a *series*—that is, as volumes related to each other by subject that are issued successively in a uniform style by the same publisher. They generally have a collective series title as well as individual titles. For example, the travel publisher Lonely Planet has a series called "City Guides," which are comprehensive, pocket-sized guides to major cities for the budget traveler. The State University of New York has several different series, all starting with the words "SUNY series"—for example, the *SUNY Series on Sport, Culture, and Social Relations* and the *SUNY Series on Urban Public Policy.*

Other hybrids may be designated as *monographic serials.* These have the same physical characteristics as monographs, but they are published regularly, usually annually. They include works such as yearbooks and annual reviews.

It is often necessary to distinguish these hybrid information packages from each other because of the different ways libraries handle them. For example, some libraries treat monographs in series as a unit and place them together on the shelves; others assign each title within the series to a separate location based on its content. Some libraries treat monographic serials as serials and allow only limited circulation or in-library use; others treat them as monographs and allow them to be freely circulated.

Other types of serials with special characteristics include *newsletters* (informal bulletins, usually circulating among people with a common interest), *house organs* (periodicals issued by a company or institution for its employees and other interested supporters or clients), and *annual reports* (descriptions of an organization's operations over the previous year, including their financial statements). You may want to read a company's annual report when seeking employment, particularly if you are being interviewed for a position with the company.

Newspapers are difficult for libraries to store, because of their folio or tabloid size and generally poor paper quality. Consequently, they are usually retained on microfilm. The major dailies are indexed for retrieval (see Chapter 17), but it may be difficult to locate information in local newspapers, unless you know the approximate date.

OTHER PRINT FORMATS

Archives and *manuscripts* are not "published" as are books and journals. *Personal papers* may include letters, diaries, laboratory notes, or various drafts of a novel or poem. *Administrative records* of organizations result from regular, continuing activities and special events. They show the development of business and industry, churches, professional associations, ethnic and cultural organizations, and clubs. The largest archives are those of local, state, and federal governments.

Microform is any printed material stored in reduced size on photographic film. It is one of the oldest miniaturization formats, developed originally in 1839 and used for sending messages by carrier pigeon during the Franco-Prussian war in the 1870s. Microform can be used for filming published or unpublished materials, either to reduce their bulk (newspapers, for example), to make them available to a wider group of users (theses and out-of-print books), or to preserve the originals of fragile materials (archival records).

Several microform packages have been developed, including *microfilm* (16-mm or 35-mm film stored on reels, in cartridges, or on cassettes) and *microfiche* (105 mm by 148 mm—or roughly 4 by 6 inch—sheets of film with eye-readable headings). *Computer output microform* (*COM*) is created directly by computer using a special camera; it is produced as microfiche for product and parts catalogs, library catalogs, and company reports.

Electronic information packages include floppy disks, hard disks, and CD-ROMs (Compact Disc-Read Only Memory). CD-ROMs have immense storage capacity; they can replace as many as 1,500 floppy disks or 250,000 printed pages. They may contain the complete text of encyclopedias, sets of books or documents, or several years' runs of finding aids such as indexes, abstracting journals, and bibliographies. Many CD-ROMs have built-in software so that their contents can be searched very effectively (see Chapter 19).

AUDIOVISUAL FORMATS

Just as 33-rpm and 45-rpm recordings replaced the old "78s," so are audiocassettes and compact discs replacing "vinyl." The overwhelming trend is now to digital recording—both compact discs (CDs) and audiotapes. CDs offer better quality sound and are more durable than the phonograph records they have replaced. Digital audiotape has yet to cater to a mass market.

Art prints often use high-quality paper and reproduction techniques to try to capture the colors and surface textures of an original work of art. *Posters* are created for public display, often advertising movies and travel or promoting sports stars and rock bands.

Although a picture may be worth a thousand words, the difficulty is that in many library collections, graphic information has not been organized effectively for retrieval. Art prints can often be retrieved only by artist or title, rather than by subject or period. Early posters and photographs may not be described accurately enough for retrieval because the people or places pictured were not originally labeled and are no longer identifiable.

Holograms are a means of recording light waves reflected from an object onto photographic film. They can sometimes be viewed as special exhibits in museums and art galleries. When placed in a laser beam, they appear as three-dimensional objects that change in perspective as viewers move around them. Non-projected holograms can be purchased as novelty items in souvenir shops and dime stores.

Digital images can be taken on a digital camera, recorded on disk, and played back on computer. They can also be downloaded from the Internet, or created from printed images using a scanner and manipulated using software such as Photoshop. Various format standards, such as .gif and .jpeg, have been developed for storing and displaying digital images.

Realia are objects, such as costumes or artifacts from people's daily lives, used in teaching about a culture or community. Along with toys, games, models, and samples of various sizes, they can pose problems for libraries, especially for access and storage. *Dioramas* are small representations of scenes with backgrounds and three-dimensional models, often viewed through a window. They are common in museums, often showing historical scenes or animals in their native habitat.

Films for projection come in a range of sizes—8-mm continuous loops, super-8 "home movies," 16-mm films, and 105-mm motion pictures. The standard for documentary and training films shown in educational institutions is usually 16 mm.

The VHS half-inch *videocassette* has become the standard, overtaking the use of the Beta half-inch and Sony U-matic three-quarter inch cassettes. *Videodiscs* are video recordings that resemble shiny, metallic long-playing records. They are played back on videodisc players using lasers.

Projection equipment for computers is now available in many universities, or it can be hired commercially. Microsoft's PowerPoint is a software program that is useful for creating projections to accompany class presentations. When reserving any projection or playback equipment, be sure to check in advance that everything is in working order and that you know how to operate it.

Digital television (*DTV*) is the umbrella term used to describe the digital television system that the Federal Communications Commission adopted in 1996. Moving from traditional analog to digital technology is achieved through advanced compression techniques that allow far more data to be packed into signals. DTV broadcasts also carry Dolby digital sound signals. The FCC has mandated that all television stations broadcast digitally by 2006. *High definition television (HDTV)* is a special form of DTV. It provides images that are crisper and sharper, with high resolution that is visually perfect and digitally precise.

Kits combine a variety of information packages on a particular topic, but they are treated as a single unit by libraries. They are common for educational or curriculum materials, and may include such items as a teacher's guide, videocassettes, overhead transparencies, activity cards, and posters.

A particular feature of a *CD-ROM* is its multimedia capacity; it can provide sound, drawings, photographs, animation, and video—from bird songs, pronunciations of foreign words, and symphony concerts to art reproductions, close-up images of insects, animated explanations of chemical processes, and film clips of world leaders making speeches. Its interactive capabilities mean that it is ideal for computer-aided instruction and other self-learning programs. Other new multimedia formats for home entertainment and education include CD-I (Compact Disc-Interactive) and DVD (Digital Versatile Disc).

In Chapter 11, we discussed interviews with experts as one of the ways to gather information. You can also gain useful information through group interaction in seminars, conferences, workshops, meetings, or informal gatherings. Notice of such meetings is often found in the newsletters and journals of relevant professional associations.

Telecommunications and computer networks are changing the way we communicate and retrieve information; they are no longer the preserve of computer buffs. The Internet, in particular, has brought computer message exchange and information access to the public. The World Wide Web, e-mail, FTP file transfer, electronic texts, electronic discussion groups, and electronic mailing lists are Internet information services used by millions of people throughout the world. They are discussed in greater detail in Chapter 21.

13

Choosing Collections and Services

Your university or college library is generally the best starting place for answering a research query. Not all academic libraries are organized in the same way, however. Some offer their services in just one location. Others have a main central library and branch libraries that concentrate on different subject areas (for example: law, health sciences, or geology) or information packages (for example: audiovisual materials, microforms, or maps).

Take advantage of library orientation tours to get to know your library. Services to note are the information desk, reference collection, OPACs (online public access catalogs), CD-ROMs, circulation desk, reserve collections, audiovisual carrels, new book displays, current periodicals and newspapers, group study areas, photocopiers, and special collections (for example: maps, government documents, curriculum materials, theses, and rare books). Reference librarians are there to help you; be sure to draw on their assistance!

It is also useful to understand what happens in libraries "behind the scenes," as libraries must carry out a number of procedures before information sources are available to users. Most libraries have *collection development policies*— that is, guidelines on what sorts of materials they should purchase in order to best serve their users.

Materials are suggested for purchase by individual professors or university departments, as well as librarians. The library carries out *verification* or bibliographic checking to be sure that they do not already own the items and that the ordering details are accurate. They may order directly from a publisher or through a library supplier, such as Baker & Taylor.

When items are received, they are processed for payment and given an *accession number*—a unique number assigned to each item sequentially in the order in which it is received and processed by the library. Staff catalog the materials, assigning subject headings (see Chapter 15) and call numbers (see Chapter 16). Materials are tagged for automated borrowing and detection by electronic security systems, and finally placed on the shelves ready for library users.

Depending on your research topic, you may want to use other libraries and information services to supplement the information sources you find in your academic library. In this chapter, we first look at a range of potentially useful collections and services, and then discuss the principles for deciding which types to approach and how to locate them.

LIBRARIES AND ARCHIVES

You are probably already familiar with school, academic, and public libraries. Most public libraries cater for local needs and interests by providing large-print books, materials in foreign languages, local history collections, or community information services. State libraries are open to the public for reference and research, and provide back-up support for public libraries. They offer special collections (for example: local history, photographs, films, or government documents) and services (business information, genealogy and family history, or online searching).

Special libraries are run by government departments and agencies, businesses, industries, and professional associations. Their primary function is to serve the employees or members of these organizations, and this is reflected in the materials they collect. They tend to specialize by subject (for example: health, art, transportation, or law). Government libraries are special libraries that serve state and federal government departments; depending on their specific responsibility, they may not be open to the public.

The Library of Congress (LC) is the largest library in the world, with over 111 million items. It assigns a high priority to collecting and preserving materials about the United States, published in the United States, or by United States citizens. Only one-third of the library's huge collection has been published in the United States, however. It has the largest collection of Russian literature outside of the former Soviet Union and a huge collection on Hispanic and Portuguese culture.

The library acquires most of its U.S. material through the copyright provisions under title 17 of the U.S. Code and the 1976 Copyright Act. This means that writers can protect their literary and other intellectual works from unauthorized use or reproduction by registering the copyright and, for published works, depositing two copies through the Library of Congress Copyright Office.

The library also provides a wide range of bibliographic services, such as printed publications and online information retrieval, and takes a leading role in promoting cooperative activities among libraries. However, its first priority is service to the United States Congress.

The National Archives and Records Administration (NARA) establishes policies and procedures for managing U.S. government records. NARA assists federal agencies in documenting their activities and makes the records of the three branches of government available to the public. Some of the interesting records available include census data from 1790, military service records, and some passenger arrival and naturalization records.

There are 12 regional archives in various parts of the country where many NARA records are available on microfilm. NARA also manages ten of the presidential libraries.

Although this doesn't include the Richard Nixon Library, NARA does maintain the Nixon archives and files. Many other types of organizations hold special collections. Some, such as churches, professional associations, and clubs, may hold historical or archival materials. Others may focus on local geographical regions or subject fields such as business and labor, children's literature, or the history of science. For example, the Folger Shakespeare Library in Washington, D.C., has over 250,000 books, films, slides, maps, and other types of information on Shakespeare and sixteenth and seventeenth century theater, history, and civilization.

Newspaper libraries clip articles or provide information online for journalists to use as background for writing stories. Braille and talking-book libraries cater to people who are blind or partially sighted. Toy libraries collect toys and games, organize them by children's developmental levels, and circulate them to parents, student teachers, and play groups.

INFORMATION SERVICES

Information services vary widely, from basic retail sales to sophisticated research. You are already familiar with many types of retail outlets selling information "products": newspaper dealers, bookstores and book exchanges, record shops, music stores (for sheet music), book and CD clubs, video and film rental firms, computer software suppliers, and Internet retailers such as Amazon.com (amazon.com) for books and Mapquest (mapquest.com) for maps.

Community information agencies, resource centers, or advisory services have been established in many communities to supply information on subjects such as youth, drugs, careers and employment, diseases such as AIDS, women's needs, family planning, consumer affairs, legal aid, building and construction, the environment, and tourism. Others are set up by government agencies to deal with health or social problems as they arise, or by business or industrial groups to promote their interests.

Most use trained staff or volunteers as intermediaries to process "raw" information and interpret it for users. Access is usually by telephone or personal visit. Information may be supplied in displays, audiovisual materials, pamphlets, or files. Some services offer personal counseling, referral to more appropriate agencies such as health or social services, or telephone "hotlines" for dealing with crises.

Corporations and government departments have public relations sections to keep target groups (including employees, clients, and the public) informed about their growth, public service, and internal developments. They supply press releases, spokespersons to handle inquiries from the media, newsletters, and annual reports. Some may also provide advisory services, displays, films and videos, and corporate sponsorships.

Online information retrieval services are offered by most research libraries, as well as by private searching firms for a fee. The former usually offer bibliographic searching of a variety of databases, while the latter concentrate more on providing commercial and financial information. Online searching is discussed in more detail in Chapter 19.

Public and commercial computer networks—of which the Internet is probably the best known—provide opportunities for finding as well as exchanging information. They enable individuals and groups to communicate by e-mail, offer opportunities through discussion groups to debate issues and exchange information, and provide protocols for transferring information files. These facilities are explained in more detail in Chapter 21. Some networks also allow users to shop, do their banking, and book airline tickets.

Press clipping services scan local and national newspapers for articles on topics specified by clients. Media monitoring services record radio and television news and current affairs programs, again for subjects or speakers specified by clients, and provide tapes or transcripts. Photography libraries provide topical photos and transparencies for advertising and publishing. Fees for such services vary.

Information brokers or professional research firms "repackage" information. Few keep collections of materials except for quick reference; they use the collections and expertise of other institutions to tailor information to their clients' specifications. They charge according to the time they spend.

Market research firms provide information "made to order" by surveying potential or actual users of products or services, and seeking their opinions. Financial analysts, such as Dun and Bradstreet, provide company backgrounds and credit ratings. "Think tanks" provide issue papers commissioned by political parties, industry associations, and other lobby groups.

FREEDOM OF INFORMATION LEGISLATION

The Freedom of Information Act came into being in 1966. This legislation requires that government departments and agencies release their records to the public on request, unless the information is specifically exempted for national security or privacy reasons.

The act also requires the departments to publish information about their organization, functions, decision-making powers, consultative arrangements, categories of documents maintained, and facilities and procedures for obtaining access to the documents.

The legislation has been used for a range of purposes, and it has been particularly useful for consumer groups and environmentalists. For example, inspection reports on a meat packing firm disclosed that it had been selling adulterated meat; legal action was taken. A tire manufacturer was forced to disclose an internal report acknowledging that a steel-belted radial tire had a tendency to lose tread; consequently the company was forced to withdraw the tire from the market.

You have the right to see any of your personal documents held by the government, no matter how long ago they were created, as well as any government documents created after July 4, 1967, and not exempt under the legislation. Consult the freedom of information officer in the appropriate government department for help with your request and details of any costs involved, or speak with the government documents librarian in your university or public library.

Most states have also enacted freedom of information legislation. Some states have also passed "sunshine" laws, which require governmental organizations to hold open meetings that have been announced in advance.

CHOOSING AMONG COLLECTIONS AND SERVICES

Having defined your topic and made a list of potential access terms (see Chapter 10), you should start your information search at your university library—either the undergraduate library or a branch library if its collection is more closely linked to your topic. If you find that the library doesn't hold enough resources, you will need to go farther afield.

When choosing which other collections or services to use, you may need to consider several factors:

- subject coverage
- size
- types of information packages
- currency of information
- availability (purchase, loan, or on-site use)
- fees or charges
- means of retrieval.

Let's look at some examples. Perhaps you have a major

essay due on social conditions related to public housing. You assume that your university library will hold relevant books and journals, but you also want to use other, more specialized collections. These include architectural firms that hold design briefs and plans for public housing they have built and government departments that have carried out social surveys of public housing tenants.

Or perhaps you have lived in Indonesia as an exchange student and are keen to get a job that makes use of your skills in the language and knowledge of political relations between the United States and Indonesia. As well as reading books, newspapers, and journals in the library, you might want to carry out regular online searches of databases, get on the mailing lists for press releases from relevant government departments, and subscribe to newsletters commenting on American-Indonesian relations.

LOCATING COLLECTIONS AND SERVICES

How do you locate the collections and services that will fulfill these wider needs? First, consult a reference librarian in your university library. Reference librarians are familiar with many other local and statewide collections. They can be particularly helpful if you have identified useful books, journals, or other sources that aren't in the library, as they can check whether other local libraries hold these materials (see Chapter 20).

You can also use directories (see Chapter 3). Consult the *White Pages* to find community services or government department libraries and public relations sections. Try the *Yellow Pages* under headings such as "Libraries," "Maps," "Films," or "Newspaper dealers."

Use specialized directories to find educational institutions or special libraries, and community directories to find associations in your area. Ask friends for suggestions. In effect, use the same skills for tracking down collections and services as you used for tracking down experts in Chapter 11.

These collections and services may have different ways of retrieving information than you're used to using in your university library. The various types of retrieval are discussed in Chapter 16.

14

Identifying Information Sources

To locate information in library collections, you need to use catalogs and finding aids. And to do this successfully, you must be able to understand and interpret the bibliographic descriptions of the information sources listed in them.

Your professors may have referred to these bibliographic descriptions as *citations* or *references*. You will also find them in the information sources you use to write term papers and assignments, and they will vary in structure as well as location. In a monograph, for example, they may appear as numbered footnotes at the bottom of a page; as numbered notes or a bibliography at the end of each chapter; or as numbered notes, a bibliography, or a reading list at the end of the text. In a journal, they may appear as brief references in the text, as numbered footnotes at the bottom of a page, or as numbered notes at the end of an article.

In Chapter 2 we discussed the way that entries in reference works are characterized by data set, set order, and style. *Bibliographic descriptions* are a special type of entry, consisting of a data set that uniquely identifies an information source. The data set is made up of data elements such as author, title, edition, publisher, and date—in effect, the information in a library catalog. One or more of the data elements—usually author, title, and subject—serve as entry headings.

When bibliographic descriptions are in electronic form, they are often called *bibliographic records*. The data elements in the records are located in particular *fields*, or parts of the record that can be identified for searching. Chapter 15 explains the strategies and techniques for locating relevant bibliographic records in catalogs, and Chapters 17 through 20 do the same for printed and electronic finding aids. Finding aids include a wide range of indexes, abstracting journals, bibliographies, and union lists.

Be careful not to confuse this new use of the term "index." In Chapters 2 through 9, it meant the index in a reference work, usually found at the back, that indicated where topics could be found within that reference work. Here *index* is defined as a separately published, systematically arranged list, giving enough information about discrete parts of information sources, as well as about the sources themselves, to identify and locate them. Indexes include printed, CD-ROM, and online resources such as *Readers' Guide to Periodical Literature* and *Social Sciences Index*. Such indexes cover not one, but dozens of information sources, and are available independently of them.

THE BIBLIOGRAPHIC DESCRIPTION

There are three steps in assessing the potential usefulness of an information source from its bibliographic description:

1. Determine whether the bibliographic description refers to the whole source or a discrete part of the source.
2. Look for the clues that indicate the information package of the source.
3. Identify each data element of the description, including the entry heading.

These steps are discussed in more detail below. Such an assessment helps you decide which collections and techniques to use to locate the information source. It also helps you narrow or focus your search if there are too many potentially useful information sources.

Once you have found the information sources you need, you must list them accurately in your own essay or assignment. The bibliographic descriptions in your footnotes or bibliography will show that you are quoting the authors' words or paraphrasing their ideas, and that you have not been copying or plagiarizing. Your bibliographic descriptions will also enable your professor to evaluate the sources you used.

The Whole Source or a Discrete Part

You must first determine whether a bibliographic description refers to the whole information source or to a discrete part of it—a journal, or an article in a journal; a book, or a chapter in a collected work or anthology; proceedings of a conference, or a paper from the proceedings; an audiocassette, or a track from the cassette.

A bibliographic description of a discrete part of an information source is called an *analytic* or *analytical entry*. In effect, it "analyzes" the contents of a source. In general, the part is described before the source itself. The clues that indicate an analytical entry, one or more of which may appear in the entry, are:

- Both an author or originator of the discrete part of the information source and an editor or compiler of the information source as a whole are named. The author or originator is usually given first in the entry, and the editor or compiler later on. The existence of an editor may be indicated by "edited by" or "ed."; of a compiler, by "compiled by" or "comp."
- Two titles are given in the entry, one for the discrete part and one for the information source as a whole.
- Pagination is indicated as a single page or range (for

example, p. 151; pp. 15–23). Note, however, that in some bibliographic descriptions for monographs, particularly in library catalogs, the total number of pages may be given (for example, 291 pp.).

- The word "in" may appear as part of the bibliographic description (Kinkaid, J.R. "Anthony Trollope and the Unmannerly Novel" in *Annoying the Victorians...*).

The Information Package

The next step is to determine the information package of the source in order to decide which collections and techniques you should use to locate it. Some types of packages are easy to recognize; others are not so obvious.

Figure 14–1 shows the data elements most commonly used in bibliographic descriptions for each type of package. Those elements unique to the particular type of package—and thus the clues that identify it—are marked with asterisks. Data elements may appear in bibliographic descriptions other than in the order listed in the figure; their order will depend on the citation styles or other conventions used.

The Data Elements

You need to be able to recognize each of the data elements in a bibliographic description to carry out your search for the information source. You can also use knowledge of these elements to help focus your search. For example, the title of a book or article briefly indicates the contents, while the title of a journal generally indicates the approach or discipline. The author and publisher help determine the authority or reputation of the work, and place of publication shows probable geographical coverage or bias. Date of publication determines currency, and pagination—in effect, the length—roughly indicates the depth of detail.

Electronic information sources are a special case, as they have all the data elements of a normal bibliographic descrip-

Figure 14–1 Data elements usually present in bibliographic descriptions of different types of information packages.

Package	Data elements
Analytic (if required)	Author of article, paper, or chapter Title of article, paper, or chapter Pages of article, paper, or chapter
Monograph	Author or corporate author, or editor or compiler of collected work Title of monograph *Edition, if other than the first *Number or frequency (for example annual, eighteenth), place, and year in which held, for conference proceedings *Publisher *Place of publication (not always given) Year of publication
Serial	Title of serial *Volume (indicated by abbreviation "vol." or as Arabic or Roman numerals set out by convention of punctuation—for example, 39: 26-47, meaning volume 39, pages 26 to 47) *Issue number (indicated by abbreviation "no.") or month of publication Year of publication
Newspaper	Title of newspaper Volume and issue (not always given) *Date of publication (day, month, and year)

Figure 14–1 *Continued*

Figure 14–1 *Continued*

Package	Data elements
Audio or visual package	Title of audio or visual package *Medium (usually in square brackets or parentheses following the title) Name of producer Year of production *Descriptive details to aid use, such as color or black and white, running time in number of minutes
Map	Title (geographic region) Publisher Place of publication (not always given) *Scale
Personal communication	Name of person Date of communication *Personal communication usually stated
Any of the packages above in electronic format	As indicated above. In addition: *Medium (usually in square brackets following the title) *Availability (information sufficient to retrieve from supplier)

*Elements that uniquely identify each information package.

tion, as well as an indication of the medium and its availability. The electronic media most likely to be cited are "CD-ROM" and "Online." The availability will vary, depending on the medium. For example, a full-text CD-ROM could be indicated as "NewsBank CD News presents the Seattle Times," and a file transferred over the Internet could be

listed as "ftp://sunsite.unc.edu/pub/docs/books/gutenberg/
etext96/mgegg10.txt."

Sometimes, additional data elements, such as the author's
affiliation, other headings under which the information
source is listed, or an annotation or abstract, make the bibliographic description even more useful. In particular, the
value of annotations and abstracts is described later in this
chapter.

IDENTIFYING PACKAGES AND ELEMENTS: SOME EXAMPLES

Let's look at a few examples of the types of bibliographic
descriptions you might come across. You will soon learn that
bibliographic descriptions are often neither complete nor
accurate. It is important, however, that you work with whatever details you have. Chapter 18 describes some of the bibliographies you can use to verify details of incomplete or
inaccurate bibliographic descriptions.

GERBERAS
   The tiny daisy that grew and grew. Gerberas. il
   Gardening 38: 58–9+ Ag '98.

This bibliographic description is an analytic entry, as there
are two titles: the title of the article ("The tiny daisy that
grew and grew. Gerberas") and the title of the journal (*Gardening*). The entry heading "GERBERAS" is the subject. No
author is indicated. The article is illustrated, indicated by
"il." You may need to use the list of abbreviations in an index to find the meaning of other abbreviations. The article
is in the August 1998 issue, volume 38 of *Gardening*, on
pages 58 to 59, plus another unspecified page or pages (indicated by "+") later on in the magazine.

Chemistry, Principles of Physical, B. COLLER,
I. R. MCKINNON & I. WILSON, $10.50. Holt.

This book has three joint authors: Coller, McKinnon, and Wilson. Its title is *Principles of Physical Chemistry*, but it has been entered in inverted word order to appear alphabetically under the word "Chemistry" as a quasi-subject heading. (It is also entered alphabetically under its title in normal word order elsewhere in the index.) The price is $10.50 and the publisher is Holt. No place or date of publication is given.

WOODS, ELDRICK (TIGER)
Tiger's greatest hits. ports.
HALE, Gordon and McKAY, Adrian.
Daily Herald, 15 Dec 1998: 18.

This entry is an analytic entry, as there are again two titles: the title of the article is "Tiger's greatest hits" and the title of the publication is the *Daily Herald*. The entry heading "WOODS, ELDRICK (TIGER)" is the subject, not the author, and portraits of Woods ("ports.") are included. Gordon Hale and Adrian McKay wrote the article, which appears in the December 15, 1998, issue of the newspaper. The article is on page 18.

The Shop on Main Street / Film Barrandov; Directors, Jan Kadar and Elmer Klos. 128 min. b & w. 1/2 in. VHS. In Czech with English subtitles. Based on the story by Ladislav Grosman.

This VHS video recording, entitled "The Shop on Main Street," is produced by Film Barrandov and directed by Jan Kadar and Elmer Klos. It is in black and white, and runs for 128 minutes. The date and place of production are not indicated, although the language (Czech) provides a clue.

ANNOTATIONS AND ABSTRACTS

Finding aids that include annotations or abstracts as part of the bibliographic description are exceptionally valuable, for they help you decide whether or not an information source is worth tracking down.

Annotations are brief commentaries that summarize the contents of an information source, point out any special features, and evaluate its potential usefulness. They appear in bibliographies, reading lists, and publishers' catalogs, as well as on book jackets and in advertisements for the publication. They most often cover fiction, non-fiction books in the arts and humanities, children's literature, films, and videos.

Annotations range from 15 to 100 words, with an average of about 60 words. They may use full sentences, but more often they use *extended phrases*—that is, incomplete sentences in which the subject of the sentence (the book, the article, the author) is implied but not stated. For example: "Gives varying views on capital punishment. Includes useful statistics. Excellent bibliography. From the series Ethics and the Law."

Indicative and Informative Abstracts

Abstracts are normally written in full sentences and summarize a work in up to 250 words. They express the intent and use the vocabulary of the author as much as possible; the abstract writer neither makes value judgments nor reveals personal opinions.

Indicative or descriptive abstracts most commonly describe discursive or lengthy texts, particularly in the humanities and social sciences, and indicate what you will find if you consult the original. They generally use the present tense and passive voice. For example: "The archeology of Mexico's Yucatan Peninsula is described, and the dates of occupation of each Mayan site are shown on an accompanying chronological chart."

Informative abstracts provide as much of the important quantitative and qualitative information as possible from the original information source and are commonly used in the sciences. They include a statement of scope or purpose, methods or treatment, equipment, results (expressed as numerical data, tables, or formulas), and conclusions. They generally use the active voice and past tense. For example: "The immobilized creatininase enzyme electrode was stable over an eight-month period and exhibited a linear response to aqueous creatinine up to 100 ppm (mg/liter), (8.8 x 10^{-4}M), in the presence of anticoagulants and endogenous compounds."

In short, indicative abstracts tell you what you will find in an information source, while informative abstracts can sometimes substitute for it. Annotations may express the views of the annotation writer rather than the author, so you should always check the original.

CITING INFORMATION SOURCES

Use Figure 14–1 in reverse to decide on the data elements to include in your footnotes or bibliography for an essay or assignment. Here the problem is determining which parts of the information source to use for bibliographic information.

For monographs, you should take details from the recto or verso of the title page (see Appendix 2 for terminology related to books), rather than the spine or outside covers. Cataloging-in-publication information can be a useful guide if it has been included. It appears in a form similar to a library catalog entry, usually on the verso of the title page.

Sometimes the identity of the data elements is not clearcut. For example, a title page may give several places of publication. Use the one that is most obvious, either because it is larger than the others, in different type, or listed first. Use the publisher, who takes responsibility for all stages of production from design to distribution, rather than the printer. Sometimes both the date of publication and the copyright date are given; use the former. If only the copyright date is given, use it, but make it clear by drawing the copyright symbol (©) before the date.

For journal articles, take the analytic details from the article itself, not the contents page of the journal, although use the latter for details about the journal. For articles that identify the author only by initials (in reference books or book reviews, for example), look up the full name in the preliminary pages. For media and electronic materials, take the details from the item itself rather than the accompanying packaging.

Always write down the exact page numbers for any sentences or paragraphs you have quoted or paraphrased. You need to include these.

The footnote system (which uses superscript numbers) and the text reference system (which briefly cites the author and date in parentheses in the text) are common for indicating the information sources used in an essay or assignment. For example, this book uses the text reference system. Your professor may tell you to use your university's style manual or one of the others listed in Figure 14–2.

The *Complete Guide to Citing Government Information Resources* supplements other style manuals by providing specific examples for citing resources of national, state, local, and regional governments, as well as many international agencies. *Electronic Styles: A Handbook of Citing Electronic Information* is useful for citing CD-ROMs, the World Wide Web, FTP, and electronic bulletin boards and discussion groups.

Figure 14-2 Publications describing styles for citing information sources.

Chicago Manual of Style: The Essential Guide for Writers, Editors, and Publishers. 1993. 14th ed. Chicago: University of Chicago Press.

Council of Biology Editors. Style Manual Committee. 1995. *Scientific Style and Format: The CBE Manual for Authors, Editors and Publishers.* 6th rev. ed. Northbrook, Illinois: Council of Biology Editors.

Garner, Diane L. and Diane H. Smith. 1993. *The Complete Guide to Citing Government Information Resources: A Manual for Writers and Librarians.* Bethesda, Maryland: Congressional Information Service.

Gibaldi, Joseph. 1998. *The MLA Style Manual and Guide to Scholarly Publishing.* 2nd ed. New York: Modern Language Association.

Harnack, Andrew and Eugene Kleppinger. 1998. *Online! A Reference Guide to Using Internet Sources.* New York: St. Martin's Press.

Li, Xia and Nancy B. Crane. 1996. *Electronic Styles: A Handbook of Citing Electronic Information.* 2nd ed. Medford, New Jersey: Information Today.

Publication Manual of the American Psychological Association. 1994. 4th ed. Washington, D.C.: American Psychological Association.

Turabian, Kate L. 1996. *A Manual for Writers of Term Papers, Theses, and Dissertations.* 6th ed. Chicago: University of Chicago Press.

15

Using Library Catalogs

L ibrary collections are organized so that, although information sources are located in only one place on the shelves according to a classification scheme, their bibliographic descriptions can be found in the catalog under numerous access terms. For each information source, the link between the classification scheme and the catalog is the call number (see Chapter 16).

PURPOSES OF LIBRARY CATALOGS

Over their long history, library catalogs have taken many forms: as manuscripts, bound volumes, cards, microfiche, and computer printouts. Now most university, public, special, and school libraries use *online public access catalogs* (*OPACS*). Regardless of the form of the catalog, its purposes remain the same. They are to:

- uniquely identify the information sources in the collection through their bibliographic descriptions
- enable these information sources to be retrieved using data elements in the descriptions as access terms—usually author, title, and subject as a minimum
- link the bibliographic descriptions to the physical locations of the information sources by indicating their call numbers.

In many respects, the process of using the catalog to find information sources in a library's collection is analogous to using the index to find information within a reference work. Catalog entries conform to a conventional structure as do index entries, although there are many more elements in their data sets.

What these purposes mean in practical terms is that most catalogs are able to show what information sources are available in the collection:

- by a particular author—for example, the novels of F. Scott Fitzgerald
- for a particular title—for example, the various versions (translated, edited, condensed, set to music, filmed, and recorded) of *Romeo and Juliet*
- about a particular subject—for example, the books, journals (but not individual journal articles), films, videos, photographs, and recordings about scuba diving.

If you are just starting your search, you will probably approach the catalog by subject, using some of the access terms you have listed for the concepts in your research topic (see Chapter 10). If you have already used some finding aids such as indexes or bibliographies (see Chapters 17 and 18), you may need to search the catalog by the author or title for the information sources you have identified.

DECISIONS IN A CATALOG SEARCH

Some library computer systems are set up to provide access to a range of information services. In addition to the library's catalog, they may include a library "bulletin board" that lists opening hours, library tours and instruction, or online databases available; a master list of borrowers that lets you know what books you have on loan, when they are due, and whether you have any outstanding fines; and a campus-wide information system with access to the Internet (see Chapter 21). If this is the case, select the library catalog from the menu.

Most library catalogs provide a printed or on-screen guide to their use. You may need to select the "Help" or "?" key to access it. To carry out a search, you start by choosing options from a series of menus; this means you can explore, as well as backtrack if you get lost. Unfortunately, however, each catalog provides different searching options and uses different commands, so it may take you a while to adapt to each catalog's idiosyncrasies.

The first few catalog screens display a welcome message and the main menu. If a screen has not been used for a few minutes, it may be blank or have a moving design as a screen saver. You normally press the enter or return key to get started. However, if someone else has been using the catalog and left off in mid-search, you may need to return to the main menu to start your own search.

In carrying out a search, you must make several decisions regarding the:

- information packages to search for
- data elements to search for
- types of access to use
- types of commands to use.

We will discuss each decision in turn. But remember, because library catalogs vary, the decisions listed here may be presented in a different order and expressed in different words than those you need to make during your search.

Information Packages

If you are looking for a particular type of information package, it saves time if you can limit your search in this way from the start. In some online catalogs, for example, you can search for all types of information packages, or alternatively, specify one of the following: journals and newspapers, maps, pictures, music, films and video recordings, oral histories and folklore, or manuscripts. In many catalogs, however, this option is available only later, as one of the ways to limit a search that has retrieved too many items.

This option is particularly useful when you are looking for journals. Because many journals have very broad geographic or subject discipline words in their titles (for example, "American," "education," or "science"), it saves the computer from having to search for these same common words across all the materials in the collection.

Data Elements

Data elements that are common in bibliographic records are indicated in the sample catalog entries for a monograph and a journal, as shown in Figures 15–1a and 15–1b, respectively. Each of the data elements is located in a particular field of the bibliographic record. To carry out a search you must decide what data element to look for. The most common options—author, title, and subject—are discussed in more detail later in the chapter.

From Figure 14–1, you are familiar with several of the data elements that are likely to appear in bibliographic records. There are a few additional ones you should learn about to interpret a catalog entry. These are:

- *uniform title*, a standardized form of a title that brings all of the catalog entries for the information source together. Uniform titles are used when an information source has appeared under various titles or could be confused with others having the same title
- *series title*, indicating that an information source is one of several issued by a publisher on a particular topic, usually in a similar format and style
- *collation*, which provides a physical description of an information source—for example, number of pages and

Figure 15–1 Typical catalog records for a monograph (a.) and a serial (b.).

a. Monograph

CALL NUMBER	RF354.94081 HOLDINGS:	2 other copies
	.C771	
AUTHOR	Cook, John, 1947–	
TITLE	A guide to Commonwealth government information sources / by John Cook, Nancy Lane, Michael Piggott.	
PUBLISHED	Sydney: Pergamon Press, 1988 ←	*Imprint*
DESCRIPTION	xii, 89 p.; 21 cm. ←	*Collation*
ISBN	0080344216 (pbk.)	
SERIES	1. Guides to Australian information sources ←	*Series title*
NOTES	1. Includes index.	
	2. Bibliography: p. 81–85.	
AUTHORS	1. Lane, Nancy D. (Nancy Diane), 1946–	
	2. Piggott, Michael, 1948–	
SUBJECTS	1. Australian Archives.	
	2. Federal government—Australia—Information services—Bibliography.	*Tracings*
	3. Government publications—Bibliography.	
	4. Government publicity—Australia—Bibliography.	
	5. Public record—Australia—Bibliography.	
	6. Freedom of information—Australia.	

Figure 15–1 *Continued*

b. *Serial*

CALL NUMBER	973.05 MIS
UNIFORM TITLE	Journal of American History (Bloomington, Ind.)
TITLE	The Journal of American History
PUBLISHED	Bloomington, Ind.: Mississippi Valley Historical Association, c1964–
DESCRIPTION	v.; 26 cm.
ISSN	0021–8723
NOTES	Vols. for June 1964–Mar. 1965 published by the Mississippi Valley Historical Association; June 1965–, by the Organization of American Historians.
SUBJECT	United States—History—Periodicals.
ORGANIZATIONS	1. Organization of American Historians.
	2. Mississippi Valley Historical Association.
ISSUES HELD	v. 51– (June, 1964–)
	Microfilm

⎫
⎬ *Tracings*
⎭

⟵ *Holdings open entry*

size in centimeters for monographs, or number of reels and running time for films
- *contents list* for collected works
- *notes* indicating the inclusion of illustrations, maps, bibliographies, and the like
- *tracings*, the additional entry headings under which an information source appears in the catalog—for example, joint authors, cover title, and subject headings
- *International Standard Book Number* (*ISBN*), a unique number assigned to each book based on the country of publication and the publisher, which is used for identification
- *International Standard Serial Number* (*ISSN*), a unique number assigned to each serial to aid identification
- *accession number*, a sequential number that a library assigns to each information source in the order it is received
- *holdings*, the copies of an information source that a library owns.

Holdings for monographs may indicate the total number of copies in the library, the various branches of the library that hold copies, or the accession number for each copy. For journals, *open entries* give a starting volume and year, followed by a dash; the expectation is that the library has continued to receive that journal. *Closed entries* give both starting and ending dates; the library holds only those volumes and issues between the inclusive dates. Some entries, either open or closed, may indicate that issues are missing.

Generally a catalog search by author automatically includes authors, editors, compilers, translators, illustrators, producers, and composers, as well as analytic entries for authors of major works in anthologies. Some catalogs may separate personal authors from corporate authors and ask you to choose one or the other. If you want books about an author, rather than by an author, you would normally search for the author's name as a subject.

A catalog search by title normally includes titles, cover titles if different from full titles, subtitles if works are known by them, titles of analytic entries for major works in anthologies, and series titles. In some catalogs, you must select this last option separately. A catalog search by subject may be limited to assigned subject headings, or there may be options to include titles, contents lists, notes, or the full record.

Depending on the catalog's software, you may be able to search by more options than author, title, and subject—for example, date, place of publication, publisher, call number, and ISBN or ISSN. Alternatively, these data elements may be used to limit a search that has retrieved too much.

In general, the more fields you search through, the more items you will retrieve. However, the more fields you search through, the more likely that some of the items you retrieve will not be useful. This relationship is explained more fully in Chapter 19.

Types of Access

When you carry out a search, you will be using one or more of the four types of electronic access—menu-driven, browse, keyword, or hyperlinked—outlined in Chapter 2. Searches usually start with menu-driven access, to enable you to make the decisions discussed above. You may then be able to choose alternative types of access:

- Browse access. This leads you to entries that begin with the search term you input, from among a "master list" of terms arranged alphabetically. Typical browse access searches are by author, first word(s) of title, or first word(s) of assigned subject headings. The steps in this type of search are shown in Figure 15–2.
- Keyword access. This focuses on terms that can occur anywhere within a field (or indeed, the bibliographic record), in any order, and often combined with other terms by a logical operator. This access is most com-

**Figure 15–2 Typical steps for a search using browse access.
Display screens are indicated by rectangles.**

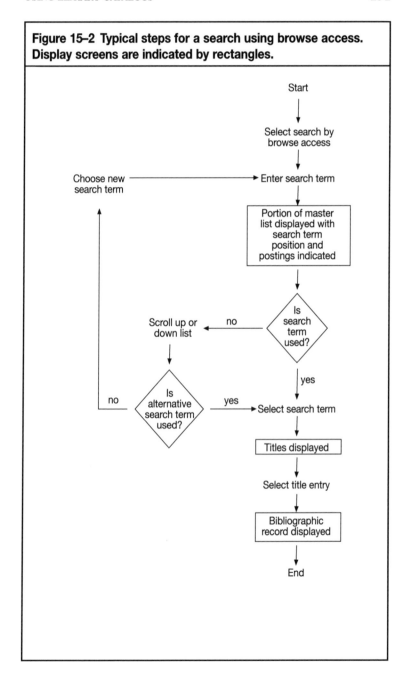

Figure 15–3 Typical steps for a search using keyword access. Display screens are indicated by rectangles.

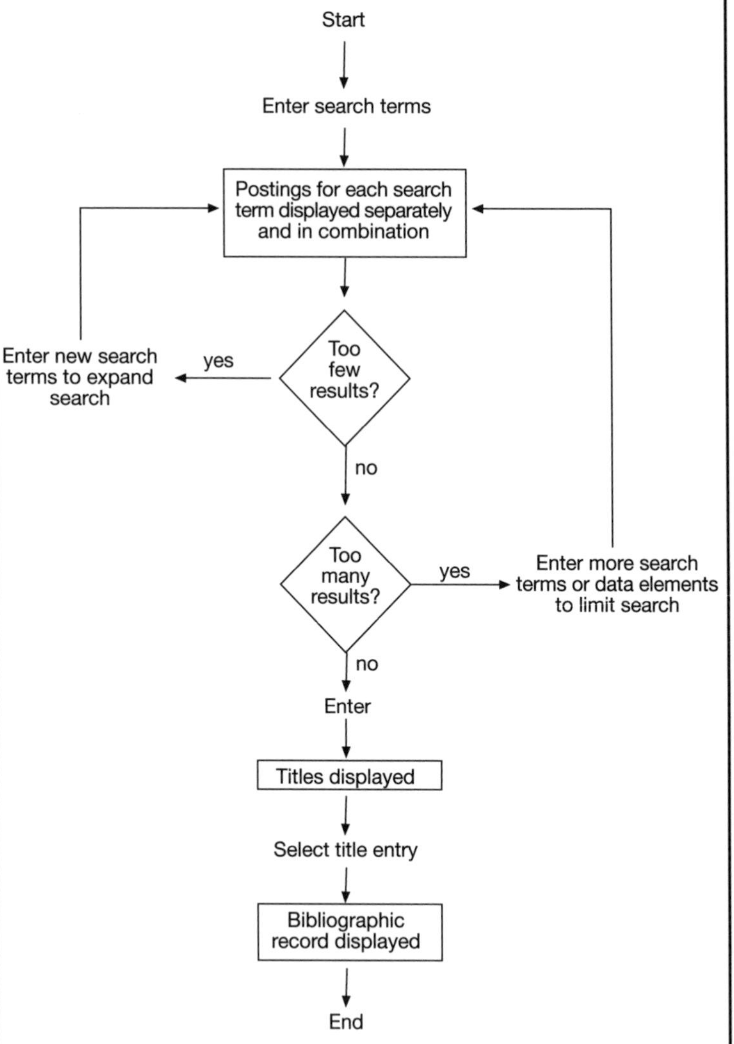

mon for searches by subject, but it is also often available for searches by title. The steps in this type of search are shown in Figure 15–3.

- Hyperlinked access. Some catalogs have commands that enable you to move directly from one bibliographic record to others with the same author, subject heading, or call number. This process is similar to hyperlinked access.

Types of Commands

Most catalogs have similar types of commands, but unfortunately, they use different keystrokes to carry them out. They generally include variations on the commands shown in Figure 15–4. Not every catalog has all these commands; others have still more. Most catalogs list the commands you are most likely to need at the bottom of each screen.

AUTHOR SEARCHES

Figure 15–2 shows the typical steps in an author search using browse access. Once you have entered the author's name as a search term, the screen displays the name in its place within the alphabetical list of authors, with *postings* (the number of information sources linked to that name). All terms are usually numbered, and the search term is marked or highlighted in some way. If the term is not in the list, the place where it would appear is usually indicated.

Having the author's name displayed within the context of the alphabetical list is useful for two reasons. First, if you are uncertain of the author's first name or initial, you can scroll up or down the list to try to find the right person. Second, many authors publish different information sources under slightly different forms of their name. These forms are often listed close to each other alphabetically, and you can easily check all of them.

Figure 15–4 Types of commands used in library catalogs.

Return to the main menu

Get help

Select a particular type of search

Input a search term or terms

Limit the search by type of information package

Limit the search by date

Select an entry heading from among those listed

Sort the list of entries into order by author

Sort the list of entries into order by title

Sort the list of entries into order by date

Display the bibliographic record for an entry heading

Go back to select another entry heading from among those listed

Display a list of information sources by the same author

Display a list of information sources with the same subject heading

Display a list of information sources with the same call number

Go on to the next screen

Return to the previous screen

Start another search of the same type

Start another search of a different type

Check the location or availability of an information source

Reserve the information source if it is out on loan

Print or download a bibliographic record

In theory, this second situation should never occur because librarians set up *authority files* to keep track of all the names and forms of name each author uses. The catalog should list all the books by an author under only one form of the name—usually the one most commonly used. The catalog uses "see" references to direct users from other forms of the name to the one used. Libraries do not always have the resources to determine if people of similar name are indeed the same person, however. For example, I go by both Nancy Lane and Nancy D. Lane; in some catalogs I have been treated as if I were two different people.

Your next step is to select one of the entries, either by typing the sequential number attached to the author's name (not the number of postings) or by highlighting the name and pressing enter. This brings up a second display that gives the titles of the information sources linked to that author's name. Select the title you are after, and the bibliographic record appears.

For example, you may have enjoyed reading *The Shipping News* and want to find other books that E. Annie Proulx has written. You select an author search and enter "Proulx, E" in the catalog, not knowing her first name. From among the "E Proulx" listings, you note the "see" reference "Proulx, E. Annie, see Proulx, Annie." You then scroll up the list to "Proulx, Annie" and press enter, which brings you to a list of titles: *Heart Songs, Accordion Crimes,* and *Brokeback Mountain*, as well as *Shipping News*. You can then highlight and enter each of these titles in turn to find the call numbers and other bibliographic details.

Some catalogs provide author searches by keyword, particularly for corporate authors. Others enable you to sort the list of titles by an author into either alphabetical or date order.

TITLE SEARCHES

You can search by title using one or more of the types of access listed. If you use browse access, the screen displays an alphabetical list of titles starting with your search terms as the initial words in the title. You can scroll up or down the list if your initial words are not sufficient to pinpoint the entry you require. A search by title is similar to the search shown in Figure 15–2, with the titles shown on the initial rather than the second display screen.

For example, you may be after Jack Kerouac's *On the Road*, but not knowing how to spell "Kerouac" for sure, you select a browse title search and enter "On the Road." The next screen displays a small portion of the alphabetical list of titles, pointing to the most likely one, with the number of different entries for each title:

	1. On the Riviera	1
	2. On the Riviera Parisian	2
→	3. On the Road	9
	4. On the Road (a collection of verse)	1
	5. On the Road Again	3

You enter the third item on the list, and the nine information sources entitled *On the Road* are displayed. A portion of this next list is as follows:

1.	On the road	(magazine)
2.	On the road	picture, ca 1850
3.	Kerouac, Jack 1922–1969 On the road	1957
4.	Kerouac, Jack 1922–1969 On the road	1979
5.	Puxon, Grattan On the road	1967

Selecting the third entry leads to bibliographic details of the first edition of the book published by Viking in 1957. Selecting the fourth entry leads to a later edition published by Penguin in 1979, which includes an introduction.

If your search is for terms that occur anywhere in the title, taken singly or combined by logical operators, you are using keyword access. In some catalogs additional fields, such as notes or contents lists, are included in keyword title searches. This type of search is similar to keyword access by subject, as shown in Figure 15–3 and discussed below. It is particularly useful when you are uncertain of an exact title.

For example, you may be a Tom Wolfe fan and would like to reread his first novel, but all you can remember from the title is the phrase "Streamline Baby." By entering these two words in a title keyword search, you will come up immediately with the bibliographic record for *The Kandy-Kolored Tangerine-Flake Streamline Baby*. You could also have taken a slightly longer route, using an author search to bring up all of his works.

In some catalogs you may also have the option of searching by exact title. In this case, you must input the full title. The problem is that, should you so much as misspell a word or leave one out, the computer is unlikely to find the information source.

SUBJECT SEARCHES

You can search by subject using one or more of the types of access listed. If you use browse access (Figure 15–2), the computer normally searches only the assigned subject headings (see the section on the *Library of Congress Subject Headings* later in this chapter). The first display screen shows the subject heading that starts with the search term, with postings, in its alphabetical place in the list of headings. You can scroll up or down the list, then select a heading by highlighting it or typing its number and pressing enter.

This brings up a second display screen showing the titles of the information sources to which the subject heading has been assigned. Some cataloging software allows you to sort this list into order by author, title, or publication date. Date order is useful if there are a lot of information sources on the subject and you want to select the most current, while alphabetical order by author is useful if you are compiling your bibliography.

For example, if you are doing a short assignment for media studies on the film noir genre and its U.S. practitioners, you might use subject browse access, entering the term "film noir." The results, with postings, might be:

→	1. Film noir	83
	2. Film noir—United States	12
	3. Film noir—United States—	
	Encyclopedias and dictionaries	2
	4. Film noir—United States—	
	History and criticism	4

By scrolling down the list of subject headings through the various subdivisions, you can often find more specific headings that will better suit your purposes. If you had selected the first heading, some of the 83 information sources listed would no doubt have been valuable. However, either of the two encyclopedias found by selecting the third heading would be sufficient to complete your assignment.

Finally, you may want to carry out a keyword search (Figure 15–3) for terms located anywhere among the assigned subject headings or, in some catalogs, anywhere in the bibliographic record. In this case, the computer carries out a search for each of the terms in turn. The first display screen often gives the number of postings for each term separately and then in combination. If you are satisfied with the results of the search, you can select a second display screen that lists the titles of the sources. If you are not satisfied, you can select other options to expand or limit the search.

For example, you may want to carry out a comprehensive search for a term paper you are writing on integrated pest management for your course in environmental studies. When you try the search term "integrated pest management" (which means that the computer is searching the list of subject headings for "integrated AND pest AND management," explained in Chapter 10), there are no results. Trying again using "integrated pests" (treated in the computer search as "integrated AND pests") results in the heading "Pests—Integrated control," with numerous additional subdivisions by country, state, congresses, dictionaries, economic aspects, juvenile literature, and so on, each listing one or more information sources when selected.

In addition, there are headings for types of pests (such as agricultural pests, insect pests, and urban pests), each subdivided first by "Integrated control" and then by the types of subdivisions listed above, each leading to one or more information sources when selected. And finally, there are numerous types of crops (apples, bananas, cotton, grapes, legumes, rice, roses, and more) used as headings, subdivided by "Diseases and pests—Integrated control," with additional subdivisions as listed above, and again leading to more information sources. So from a false start of finding no headings, the search has resulted in an overwhelming number of relevant headings.

HINTS ON SEARCHING BY AUTHOR AND TITLE

Catalogs usually use access terms that lead to the whole source, not its parts—books, not chapters in books; conference proceedings, not papers in the proceedings; journals, not articles in journals. When you use the catalog, you must be sure to search for the access term that applies to the source as a whole, not to any of its parts, even though you may only be after the part.

The way authors' names have been treated by catalogers has changed. Under older cataloging rules, the full and real names of authors were used as entry headings. Samuel Langhorne Clemens was used rather than Mark Twain, for example. This practice has changed, and now an author's most common name is used as an entry heading. Catalogs should include "see" references to guide users from one form of the name to another, but may not always do so.

Corporate bodies used as either author or subject headings can pose problems. Corporate entry headings may consist of the name of an organization, a higher body of which it is a part, the government jurisdiction under which it falls, or the name of the place in which it is located.

In general, if an organization is part of a national or state government jurisdiction, and if that jurisdiction is not included in the name of the organization, then the entry heading is in the form: "Name of state or country. Name of organization." For example, the Wildlife Management Division for the State of Washington would be entered as: "Washington (State). Wildlife Management Division." If the name of the government jurisdiction appears in the name of the organization, however, the organization is entered as it is. Thus, you will find "Washington Technology Center," not "Washington (State) Technology Center."

There can also be problems with acronyms. Some are entered as single words, while others are entered with spaces or periods between each letter. If you are unsuccessful using one method, try the other. Or better yet, try both, as there may be items listed by both!

If you have already located an information source that seems particularly relevant, some catalogs provide commands that offer direct (similar to hyperlinked) access to other information sources either by the same author, with the same subject headings, or with the same call number. This is a particularly useful and time-saving feature.

LIBRARY OF CONGRESS SUBJECT HEADINGS

The Library of Congress has developed a list of subject headings, based on its collection, to standardize terms used for subject access in library catalogs. This saves librarians from having to make up and keep track of their own headings. The *Library of Congress Subject Headings* (*LCSH*) includes the accumulated headings, revised at regular intervals, that have been established since 1898.

The policy of the Library of Congress is to make its subject headings as specific as possible. The current edition of *LCSH* lists more than 239,000 headings and more than 225,000 references from terms not used to the appropriate headings. Between 6,000 and 8,000 new headings are added each year.

It is quite arbitrary as to how some headings are entered or subdivided. For example, the subject heading chosen by the Library of Congress is "France—History," rather than, say, "French history," "History—France," or "History, French." Often, there is no consistency. Having worked out a pattern, you may find that it does not always follow: for example, "School libraries," but "Libraries, special."

LCSH uses several conventions. Entry headings that can be used in catalogs are listed alphabetically in bold type. "See" references appear alphabetically in the same list in standard type, with the note "USE Entry heading."

The relationships among entry headings and other access terms in *LCSH* are illustrated in Figure 15–5. Indented under each entry heading are all the access terms related to it in some way:

- The terms *not* used, for which the entry heading is the one chosen, follow the symbol UF (used for). These are usually variant spellings, variant forms of expression, alternative constructions, and earlier forms of headings that have been updated. The UF references are entered in catalogs as "see" references.

Figure 15–5 The relationships and conventions applied to headings in the *Library of Congress Subject Headings*.

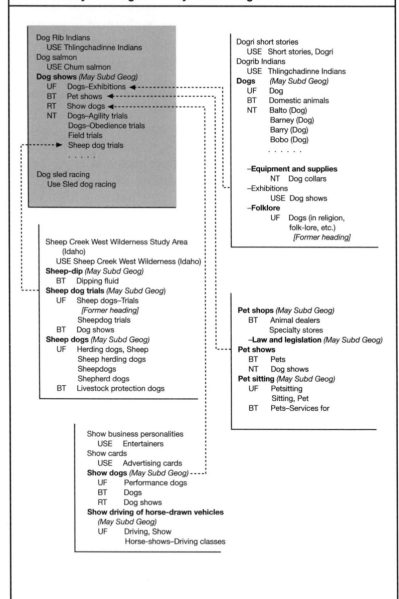

- Broader topics (BT), narrower topics (NT), and related topics (RT) indicate useful cross references. BT and NT are reciprocal (in the same way that USE and UF are reciprocal), and RT is reciprocal with itself.

LCSH also specifies how headings may be subdivided. This includes by topic (for example, "Women—Employment"), by form (for example, "Music—Catalogs" or "Fashion—Pictorial works"), by date (often following the subdivision "History"), and by geographic location.

Not all entry headings are included in *LCSH*. Those omitted include individuals, gods, corporate bodies, places and regions, zoological and botanical names, physical features, and chemical compounds.

When might you want to use *LCSH*? Unfortunately, not all catalogs have good "see" referencing. If your catalog lacks this feature and you cannot find a search term that yields results, then use *LCSH* to find the entry heading used. Or if you have a complex or detailed search to carry out, go to *LCSH* first. It provides an overview of the headings on your topic, showing their relationships clearly.

LCSH also provides scope notes, which briefly describe or define the way headings are used. For example, under the heading "Mexican Americans in motion pictures," the scope note indicates that this covers their portrayal in movies. Works dealing with their involvement in filmmaking is entered under "Mexican Americans in the motion picture industry."

HINTS ON SEARCHING BY SUBJECT

Most academic and public libraries use *LCSH*, although some school libraries and special libraries use other lists as a standard. When you have determined which subject headings are used in your university library catalog, you can assume with reasonable confidence that the same headings will be used in other university and public library catalogs.

When you carry out a subject search specifying different types of access (for example, browse or keyword) or different fields (title, subject headings, or full record), you can come up with quite different results, as illustrated in Figure 15–6. In general, the more parts of the bibliographic record you search and the broader the type of access you use, the more items you are likely to find.

If your goal is a comprehensive list of information sources relevant to your topic, you should use several kinds of searches, trying all different combinations of the possible access terms you listed in Chapter 10. You should also note the subject headings listed as tracings in the bibliographic records of the information sources you find. Add any relevant new headings to your list of access terms.

For example, after visiting the Yucatan in Mexico, I was interested in identifying all the resources available on Mayan art. I found more than 25 subject headings that were useful, each retrieving slightly different sets of information sources. I won't list all the headings, but in general I combined "Mayas," "Indians of Mexico," or "Indians of Central America" with terms related to art, such as "Antiquities," "Painting," "Sculpture," or "Pottery."

Finally, be aware that when you are searching, particularly by keyword, you may well get some erroneous results. For example, when searching for Mexican pottery, I got several listings that included pottery from New Mexico.

For searching online catalogs, my motto is always: Look under all possibilities.

Figure 15–6 A comparative search of one library catalog, indicating how the selection of different fields and different types of access using singular and plural terms can yield very different results.

Search term	Fields searched	Type of access	Number of titles listed	Number of LC subject headings listed*	Typical title or subject heading retrieved
Airplane	Title	Browse access, initial position	11		Airplane Transport
Airplanes	Title	Browse access, initial position	3		Airplanes of the World
Airplane	Title	Keyword access, any position	149		Controlling the Airplane in Skywriting
Airplanes	Title	Keyword access, any position	80		A Guide to European Airplanes
Airplane	Subject	Browse access, initial position		18	Airplane racing—Australia
Airplanes	Subject	Browse access, initial position		453	Airlines, Military—Flight testing
Airplane	Subject	Keyword access, any position		93	Survival after airplane accidents, shipwrecks, etc.—Personal narratives
Airplanes	Subject	Keyword access, any position		575	Fokker airplanes—History

*These subject headings would each have one or more titles listed; in some cases, however, several of these headings could be assigned to the same title.

16

Retrieving Information Sources

L ibraries use *classification schemes* to place information sources into logically related, systematically arranged groups of subjects. Theoretically, such schemes should bring together all information sources on a given subject. This does not happen in reality, however, because some sources cover several different subjects, but they can be in only one place at a time.

This is one of the reasons why the catalog is necessary. Even though both the classification scheme and the catalog provide access to the collection by subject, the catalog complements the classification scheme. It serves as an index to the scheme.

Call numbers (explained later in this chapter) assign numbers from a classification scheme to information sources as they are added to the collection so that they can be placed in a unique but *relative position* to each other. The sources on either side may change as new items are added and old ones removed.

This contrasts with placing sources in a *fixed position* or specific place on a shelf, a position to which they are always returned. This practice was common in libraries during the Middle Ages when, because of their value, manuscripts were sometimes chained to the shelves. You can still see chained books in some of the historical college libraries at Oxford and Cambridge.

Many libraries assign an accession number to each item

they acquire so that they can keep track of it in the collection. A few store some parts of their collection, such as films, in accession number order. Most libraries do not use the accession number for physical organization, however, but for keeping track of the size of their collection, stocktaking, or enabling students to reserve particular items.

Most library materials are held in *open stacks* that are accessible to all users. Libraries may hold certain types of materials, such as reserve books, theses by graduates of the university, or rare books, in collections accessible only to staff. These are called *closed stacks*.

Most academic libraries separate their audiovisual from their print materials. Some also separate their journals from their monographs. Some public and school libraries, however, maintain *integrated collections*—that is, collections in which information sources are shelved sequentially in call number order, regardless of the type of information package.

The two most common schemes for classifying information sources are the Dewey Decimal Classification (DDC) and the Library of Congress (LC) Classification. You are most likely to find the DDC in school and public libraries, and the LC Classification in academic, special, and research libraries.

DEWEY DECIMAL CLASSIFICATION

The DDC was devised by Melvil Dewey in 1873 and has endured many revisions. It divides knowledge into ten main groups or classes. Remembering these basic groups helps you find your way around most public libraries. As a way of remembering them, think of the scheme like this:

000 *Generalities* includes the professions (librarianship, journalism) and research tools (particularly reference works) developed to help record human progress.

100 *Philosophy and related disciplines* includes attempts to understand our basic existence, knowledge, and experience. From here, we have turned to

200 *Religion* as a further explanation of life and to add meaning to it. Then, with

300 *Social sciences*, we have begun to investigate our relationships with each other.

400 *Language* allows us to communicate the ideas we have developed. We have progressed to

500 *Pure science* by studying nature and seeking explanations for the phenomena we have observed, and then applied these natural laws as

600 *Technology and applied science*, allowing us to manage our environment. With increasing control, we have had more time to develop

700 *Arts and recreation* to enrich our lives, and

800 *Literature*, to reflect upon and interpret our experiences. Finally, we have recorded the

900 *History* of events and individuals (biography), and *Geography*, as our knowledge of other places and peoples has expanded.

From using libraries, you know that these ten groups are broken down further into 1,000 three-digit numbers followed by decimal fractions, so that various aspects of a subject can be specifically expressed. This arrangement accommodates three important features of DDC: organization by discipline, by hierarchy, and mnemonically.

Different aspects of a subject are included in the scheme within the relevant *discipline*. Food, for example, may appear in a variety of disciplines, as shown below:

Subject: Food	**DDC**	**Discipline**
Allergies	616.975	Medical sciences
Chains	577.16	Life sciences
Commercial processing	664	Chemical engineering

Cooking	641.5	Home economics
Food supply for spacecraft	629.4773	Engineering
Product safety	363.192	Social problems and services
Taboos	394.16	Customs, etiquette, folklore

The breakdown of the DDC into divisions with several levels of subdivisions results in a *hierarchical* structure such that each subdivision is a subset of, or contained within, the term or concept at the next highest level. For example:

617.7523	Contact lenses, is a subset of
617.752	Optical work, is a subset of
617.75	Disorders of refraction and accommodation, is a subset of
617.7	Ophthalmology, is a subset of
617	Miscellaneous branches of medicine/surgery, is a subset of
610	Medical sciences/medicine, is a subset of
600	Technology (Applied sciences).

Finally, DDC is a *mnemonic* scheme (when pronounced, the initial "m" is silent), which means that it has built-in memory aids. For example, whenever possible each country is given a constant number in the scheme. Thus:

France	44	History of France 944
		Geography of France 914.4
Japan	52	History of Japan 952
		Geography of Japan 915.2
Australia	94	History of Australia 994
		Geography of Australia 919.4

DDC numbers are placed on the shelves in numerical order, treating the digits following the decimal point as decimal fractions, as illustrated in Figure 16–1.

Figure 16–1 Examples of Dewey Decimal Classification and Library of Congress Classification numbers listed in order as they would be placed on a shelf.

Dewey Decimal	Library of Congress
629	Q81 .A1
629.1	QA76 .A79
629.12	QA76 .A8
629.13	QA76.5 .B296
629.13092	QA76.5 .B3
629.132	QA76.5 .B33
629.1323	QA76.9 .S8.C6
629.132322	QA76.9 .S88.D46
629.133	QA76.9 .S88.D5
630	QA76.9 .S9.D36

LIBRARY OF CONGRESS CLASSIFICATION

The Library of Congress (LC) Classification Scheme was developed by the library, starting in 1898, to organize its own collection. The scheme is being continually revised to keep up with the expansion of knowledge.

The main LC classes are based on letters of the alphabet rather than numerals, which allows the division of knowledge into 26 fields rather than ten. LC has thus far used 21 main classes, which are outlined in Figure 16–2. They may initially be subdivided by a second letter (although not all are), then by numerals (up to four places, rather than three), and finally by both letters and numerals after the decimal point.

Letters and numbers that precede the decimal sign are treated in their normal alphabetical or numerical order. Those that follow the decimal sign are treated as decimal fractions. The order of LC classification numbers is illustrated in Figure 16–1.

Figure 16–2   The 21 main classes of the Library of Congress Classification scheme.

A   General works

B   Philosophy, psychology, and religion

C   History: archaeology, archives, genealogy, and collective biography

D   History: Great Britain, Europe, Asia, Africa, and Australia

E-F History: North and South America

G   Geography, anthropology, folklore, sport, and recreation

H   Social sciences

J   Political science

K   Law

L   Education

M   Music

N   Fine arts

P   Language and literature

Q   Science

R   Medicine

S   Agriculture

T   Technology

U   Military science

V   Naval science

Z   Bibliography and librarianship

CALL NUMBERS

The *call number*, usually found at the bottom of the spine of books and bound journals and in the top left corner of catalog entries, is used to assign a unique relative position to each information source in a collection. It consists of a *notation* (letters, numbers, or other symbols), often in three parts.

The first is a symbol indicating that the source may be in a special area (for example, "AV" for audiovisual or "REF" for reference) or on a special shelf because of its size. The second part of the call number is the classification number already described. The third is the *Cutter number*, a numerical shorthand used to give each source a unique location within any given classification number, based on the author's last name. The Cutter number is taken from a table invented by Charles Ami Cutter, in which figures are arranged after each initial letter so that names fall alphabetically. Thus Nancy Lane would be .L266, falling between, say, Lambert, .L222 and Langer, .L276.

USING THE CATALOG AND CLASSIFICATION SCHEME TO ADVANTAGE

If your intention in a library is browsing, you need never approach the catalog. Knowing the main classes of the classification scheme enables you to browse the shelves in the subject areas in which you're interested.

The classification scheme can also be used in conjunction with the library catalog to good effect. If you already have a relevant book on your topic, you can look it up in the catalog by author or title, note the classification number, and then look on the shelves for other books with the same number. Some catalogs have a command that enables you to display the titles with call numbers falling to either side of this book; you can also scroll further in either direction by using the arrow keys or page up and down.

If you have a short deadline (that is, you do not care how many books the library may have on a topic—you want the ones on the shelves and you want them now), you can look up the topic in the subject catalog, copy down the classification numbers occurring most frequently, and browse the shelves at those numbers to see what is available.

Some libraries may shelve different types of information packages—for example, films or kits—in different places. Others may also shelve different size books separately to save space in the stacks: normal-size or *quarto* books (assembled from printed sheets folded four times for cutting), the larger *folios* (folded only twice), and the smaller *octavos* (folded eight times). You must remember to browse the classification numbers in each of these areas to find all the information sources available on a topic.

If you have enough time, the most effective way of using the catalog is to look for information sources by subject or, if you already have some leads, by author or title. Print out the records if the catalog is attached to a printer or else copy down the authors, titles and call numbers to search for these sources on the shelves. If they are on loan, you can reserve them.

There is no one right way to use a catalog and classification scheme. Pick the way that seems best for the research topic you are working on and the amount of time you have available.

OTHER MEANS OF RETRIEVAL

Information services other than libraries may use less sophisticated means of organizing their materials, and consequently, require less sophisticated means of retrieval. Many retail outlets, such as news dealers, bookstores, video rental firms, record stores, and computer software suppliers, may organize their materials by information package, age level, or genre. Although they may use computers for their stock control, customers depend on either browsing or self-indexed retrieval to find what they want.

Browsing

Information packages provide a rough and ready way to organize materials. News dealers may display their newspapers in piles, magazines on shelves with covers displayed, and books on revolving stands. Record stores may separate audiocassettes, audiocassette singles, and compact discs. You may have imposed a similar rudimentary order on your home library—perhaps with paperback fiction on the top shelf, texts on the next, and basic reference works on the bottom.

These outlets may also organize their materials by age level or other characteristics. News dealers may separate fiction from non-fiction, or children's books from adult books. Video rental stores may separate tapes by their classification (for example, children's, general, or restricted) or by the cost of renting.

These outlets may further group their materials by genre or broad subject. In bookstores, fiction may be grouped in genres such as mystery and detective, romance, science fiction, and Westerns. Non-fiction may be grouped by broad subjects such as cooking, gardening, health, travel, and philosophy. Record stores may group their collections by musical styles such as classical, folk, or rock. Video rental firms may group their tapes by comedy, drama, new releases, or science fiction. Directional signs, shelf labels, floor plans, and similar guides are used to help you find what you are looking for.

Sometimes information sources within these groups are placed in order for self-indexed retrieval, but sometimes they are placed beside each other quite randomly. This is a highly inefficient way of retrieving materials, although it is conducive to serendipity—the luck of finding just what you need when you may not be looking for it. But you can never depend on serendipity!

Self-indexed Retrieval

Information sources may be more readily retrieved if they are placed in alphabetical order in relation to each other, based on one of the data elements—usually the author, but sometimes the title. This is called *self-indexed retrieval*.

After an initial grouping by information package, age level, or genre, there is usually a subsidiary alphabetical arrangement. Many bookstores, school libraries, and public libraries organize their fiction by the surnames of the authors. Often record stores use the names of recording artists and video rental firms use the titles of movies to organize their stock, while libraries use the titles to shelve their new periodicals. Special libraries and community information services may arrange their files by still other data elements: clients, agencies, projects, or subjects such as ethnic groups, diseases, or social problems.

With self-indexed retrieval, information sources are readily available as long as they are maintained in proper order. Difficulties arise, however, when the data element by which an information source is organized can take more than one form; you may not know which is the one used. For example, a file about HIV and AIDS may be located under either of the two acronyms or either of the two names spelled out in full. Difficulties also arise when you want to search for a data element other than the one used for organization— for example, if paperbacks are organized by author, but you only know the title.

RETRIEVAL OF ARCHIVAL MATERIALS

Archival materials are not organized by their subject content, but according to the principles of provenance and original order. *Provenance* refers to the preservation of the context of the records—their links to the purpose, function, and activities of the agency that created them. The records of each agency or activity are kept intact and treated as an integral unit. *Original order* requires that the records be retained in the order in which they were created, maintained, or used, and not rearranged according to some imposed order.

In general each collection is assigned a registration number. Within a collection, files are arranged and described collectively in *numbered series* (records that have been brought together in the course of their active life to form a discrete sequence), rather than as individual items, according to the agency's structure and functions. The concept underlying most archival finding aids is that you must match your subject interests against an agency's structure and functions to identify the appropriate series of records for retrieval.

17

Using Indexes and Abstracting Journals

In Chapter 2 you learned that there are two kinds of reference works: those that contain information and those that lead you to other sources containing information. The latter includes indexes, abstracting journals, bibliographies, and union lists, which are referred to collectively as *finding aids*. They may be printed, on CD-ROM, or online.

Finding aids are similar to, yet different from, catalogs. Like catalogs, they contain bibliographic descriptions of information sources. Unlike catalogs, they do not usually provide call numbers: their role is to confirm the existence of information sources, but not their location. In the special case where finding aids do indicate the locations of information sources, they are called *union lists*. Also unlike catalogs, finding aids usually list discrete parts of information sources—in particular, articles in journals, papers in conference proceedings, articles in newspapers, chapters by different authors in anthologies, and so on.

The various types of finding aids are similar to, yet different from, each other as well. Some concentrate on discrete parts of only one type of information package, particularly journals or newspapers. Others cover a range of information packages, listing some sources as a whole and discrete parts of others.

Because of their importance, four chapters in this book are devoted to finding aids. This chapter covers printed indexes and abstracting journals, Chapter 18 covers bibliographies,

Chapter 19 describes the use of finding aids on CD-ROM and online, and Chapter 20 deals with union lists and their role in inter-library lending.

VALUE OF JOURNAL ARTICLES

Indexes and abstracting journals provide a gateway to the contents of journals. There are a number of reasons why you may want to use this type of information source:

- Most experimental results, discoveries, technological developments, and medical breakthroughs first appear as journal articles, especially in scientific fields where knowledge is expanding rapidly. It may take years for this information to be published as a monograph, and some of it may never be. Therefore, journal articles are essential for keeping up with developments and locating current information.
- Journal articles are a good source of specific examples to illustrate general points you may be making in an essay or assignment. If, for example, you are writing an essay on earthquakes, you may have used several books to explain how they form and what should be done to prepare for them. But newspaper or journal articles can give you a specific example to use, say the impact of the 1994 earthquake in Northridge, California.
- There is often more choice and better availability of journals than monographs. All the monographs on a topic may already be on loan with no time to recall them, or perhaps only a few are available and you need more variety. This is when journal articles are important.
- Most authors of journal articles include references, often to other journal articles. These leads can be very useful if you need more information.

With the ever-increasing number of journals being published in many subject areas, it can be difficult to locate relevant articles on a topic. Indexes and abstracting journals make this task easier. Since indexes and abstracting journals each cover many journals, it is far quicker to search through them than through the contents pages of individual journals. This is true even if you already know which journals are most likely to cover your topic.

There is a problem, however: not all libraries hold all the journals indexed. You are bound to identify articles you know would be ideal, but find that your library does not hold them. Many libraries will obtain journal articles for you via inter-library loan (see Chapter 20), although it may take several days to get them. Some libraries are now providing electronic delivery, and this will become more common in the future.

INDEXES

Indexes to periodicals may be either general, covering a wide range of topics, or specialized, concentrating on one discipline. The most widely used general index is the *Readers' Guide to Periodical Literature*, published by the H. W. Wilson Company. Also well known is *Public Affairs Information Service (PAIS) International in Print*, which covers public affairs worldwide and indexes information sources in six languages. Both are available in print, CD-ROM, and online.

There are hundreds of specialized indexes. They include, for example, *Education Index*, *Art Index*, *Library Literature*, *Social Sciences Index*, *Humanities Index*, *General Science Index*, *Applied Science and Technology Index*, and *Business Periodicals Index*.

Indexes are published at regular intervals, often monthly. *Cumulative* volumes—that is, those that combine new entries with those of earlier issues—are published at longer intervals, usually quarterly or annually. There may, for example, be separate January and February issues of an index, followed by a March issue combining the listings in these two earlier issues with the new listings for March. The January and February issues can then be discarded.

The four essential features of reference works (see Chapter 2) also apply to indexes. Once you have had a little practice, you will find indexes easy to use. The process of using indexes is set out in sequence below, although you will probably repeat many of these steps as you discover new indexes or come across additional access terms.

1. Determine the most appropriate indexes to consult (discussed later in this chapter).
2. Select the year or years of the index that seem most appropriate to your query. There is always some time lag between events and the publication and listing of articles about them, and this varies from one index to another. For current information, begin with the most recent issue and work backwards through older issues until the information becomes too dated. For a particular period, begin with the first issue after that date and work forward. Commentators often look back on events in anniversary years (say 10 or 25 years later); these volumes may yield many reflections.
3. Look up the access terms you listed as possibilities during the second step of your search strategy (see Chapter 10). Entry headings are arranged alphabetically by author and subject, sometimes in two separate lists of entries and sometimes combined in one. "See" and "see also" references are usually included. The broader subject headings may be subdivided in much the same way as in the *Library of Congress Subject Headings* (see Chapter 15). Some indexes may include additional data elements as access terms—for example, title, important words in the title, chemical compounds, geographical regions, or genera and species.

4. Copy down the details of the relevant entries. If you need help in interpreting them, the introduction to the index should include a key to the contents of an entry, a list of abbreviations and their meanings, and a list of abbreviations of journal titles giving full titles and often addresses. To review the data elements normally included in an entry, see Chapter 14.

5. Check for further entries in the index using the same or related headings, in earlier or later volumes as appropriate. Keep a note of the indexes you have searched and their dates, as well as the access terms you have used, so that you do not go over the same ground twice.

6. Once you have a reasonable number of references, search the catalog by title to see whether the library holds the journals and issues you want. If the option is available, select a search of serials only, as it will save time. Remember to look under the title of the journal, not the author or the title of the article.

7. Check that the library's holdings include the issues you need, note the call numbers for the journals, and search for them on the shelves.

Now let's work through an example. Suppose you are writing an essay for a class in politics or twentieth century American history on the fall of the Nixon administration in August, 1974. First, try volume 34, 1974, of the *Readers' Guide to Periodical Literature*, which covers March 1974 to February 1975. Look under the heading "Nixon, Richard Milhous," subheading "Resignation," to get national viewpoints, and under "Watergate case" for related articles. Your problem here is omitting what you do not want, rather than not being able to find enough.

Next look at *PAIS International in Print* for 1974 and 1975 (these volumes cover October of one year to September of the following year). Use the headings "Nixon, Richard Milhous" and "Watergate incident, 1972" to see what was written about the event in more scholarly publications, including some international ones. To see how commentators viewed the event with the passage of time, try the 1994 volume (the year of Nixon's death) or the 1999 volume (25 years since his resignation).

ABSTRACTING JOURNALS

Abstracting journals are even more helpful than indexes, for they provide abstracts (see Chapter 14) along with the bibliographic descriptions of the journal articles. The abstracts can help you decide which articles are worth tracking down. There are abstracting journals in a wide range of broad disciplines and specialist fields: *Psychological Abstracts, Sociological Abstracts, Geographical Abstracts, Library and Information Science Abstracts, Sage Urban Studies Abstracts, World Agricultural Economics and Rural Sociology Abstracts,* and both *Women Studies Abstracts* and *Studies on Women Abstracts,* to name just a few.

Although entries in abstracting journals may be more helpful than those in indexes, searching for them is a two-step process. Bibliographic descriptions in abstracting journals are usually arranged by broad subjects, rather than alphabetically, to enable regular users to keep up-to-date by scanning the subjects in which they are interested. Access by specific topic, author, or other data elements is through an index. To use an abstracting journal, proceed as follows:

1. Determine the most appropriate abstracting journals to consult (discussed later in the chapter).
2. If you are interested in a broad subject, look in the table of contents to see where this subject is treated. Then refer to the pages in the main list of entries and browse through the bibliographic description and abstract for each article.
3. If you are interested in a specific topic, use the alphabetical index to look it up. The index indicates the lo-

cation, usually a number or code that has been assigned to each entry, but occasionally the page number. Use this number to find the entry in the main list of entries.

4. Continue from step four in the procedure for using indexes, applying the steps to abstracting journals instead.

To illustrate the use of an abstracting journal, let's continue our search for information on the fall of the Nixon administration using volume 25 of *International Political Science Abstracts*, which covers journals received from December 1974 to November 1975. In the subject index under "Watergate affair," there is a "see" reference to "United States of America," subheading "Watergate Affair." Here are listed 21 abstract numbers (see Figure 17–1). By looking these up in numerical order in the main list of entries, you can find the full bibliographic descriptions and abstracts. You would also want to look under "Nixon, Richard Milhous," subheading "Resignation, views on."

Readers' Guide Abstracts, which supplements the *Readers' Guide to Periodical Literature*, is an exception to the normal two-step procedure for locating abstracts. It lists abstracts alphabetically by specific subject headings in the same way the index does.

KWIC INDEXES

KWIC stands for "keyword in context." Each important word in a title is shown in its appropriate place in alphabetical order, as well as in relationship to its place in the title. Such an index is also called a *permuted* index. The concept can be illustrated by starting from the point of view of the indexer rather than the user.

For an article entitled "A Comparison of the Mass Media in Canada and the United States," the indexer would determine all of the important words in the title under which a user might look for such an article. These are "Compari-

Figure 17–1 Subject index (with locations listed under the entry heading "United States of America," subdivision "Watergate affair") and related abstract in volume 25, 1975, of *International Political Science Abstracts.*

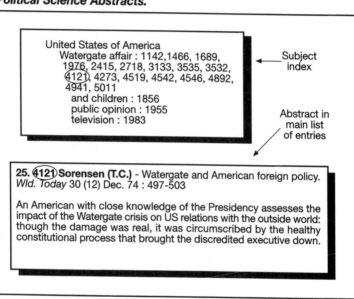

United States of America
   Watergate affair : 1142, 1466, 1689,
    1976, 2415, 2718, 3133, 3535, 3532,
    4121, 4273, 4519, 4542, 4546, 4892,
    4941, 5011
    and children : 1856
    public opinion : 1955
    television : 1983

Subject index

Abstract in main list of entries

25. **4121** **Sorensen (T.C.)** - Watergate and American foreign policy. *Wld. Today* 30 (12) Dec. 74 : 497-503

An American with close knowledge of the Presidency assesses the impact of the Watergate crisis on US relations with the outside world: though the damage was real, it was circumscribed by the healthy constitutional process that brought the discredited executive down.

son," "Mass," "Media," "Canada," and "United States." The title and all the information about it—author, journal, volume and issue, year, and pages—would appear five times in the index. The title would appear in alphabetical order, interspersed with all of the other title entries in the index, as follows:

> Canada and the United States, Comparison of the Mass Media in
>
> Comparison of the Mass Media in Canada and the United States
>
> Mass Media in Canada and the United States, Comparison of the
>
> Media in Canada and the United States, Comparison of the Mass

United States, Comparison of the Mass Media in
   Canada and the

The "indexer" in many permuted indexes is not a person
but a computer. The computer is instructed to ignore a list
of *stop words*—that is, words that convey no information or
that people are unlikely to look up, such as "of," "the," "in,"
or "and"—and then to print out in alphabetical order all of
the titles in their natural as well as their permuted word
orders.

A permuted index has two advantages for users: there are
several access terms by which a title can be located, and the
terms are expressed in the same language as used by the author. There are also two disadvantages. First, if the author
has used a vague or clever title that does not indicate the
contents of an article, it may never be found in the index.
Some permuted indexes augment titles with terms selected
from the contents to try to overcome this problem. Second,
if different authors have used different terms to express the
same concept, users of permuted indexes must look under
all of these terms or they are likely to miss information.

Occasionally, even singular and plural word forms may
be located far apart in a permuted index. If, for example, you
are interested in the use of radio as opposed to television,
there may be numerous titles listed under the terms "radio"
and "radios." But these may be pages apart, because articles
containing the words "radioactivity," "radioastronomy," "ra-
diocarbon dating," "radiofrequency," "radiography," "radio-
isotope," and "radionavigation" would intervene.

Remember that in normal indexes and abstracting journals
the indexers have chosen the entry headings for you. They
have brought all relevant articles together under these headings, regardless of the words in the titles. In permuted indexes there is no control over the terms used. You may have
to search under all conceivable terms that have been used
in titles describing your topic to find the articles you need.

CITATION INDEXES

Citation indexes operate on a completely different principle from the other indexes discussed so far, which assume that you are looking for information by subject or author. Citation indexes assume that you already have an article central to your topic. You can find older material by using the references in the article, but how can you find newer material—that is, works by authors who have cited the article since its publication? That's where citation indexes are of value.

The best-known citation indexes, produced by the Institute for Scientific Information (www.isinet.com), are the *Science Citation Index*, the *Social Sciences Citation Index*, and the *Arts and Humanities Citation Index*. All are computer produced and relatively expensive because of their wide coverage. They are, therefore, generally available only through larger university and research libraries, either in printed form or online.

The procedures for using a citation index are as follows:

1. Look up the author and title of the article (longer names may be truncated), starting with the same volume as the year of its publication and continuing forward in time. For example, if the article was published early in 1992, look in the citation index from 1992 to the present. If the article was published in November or December, 1992, you may as well start with 1993.
2. Remember that you are searching for articles in which authors have cited the article as a reference. In the social sciences, it is less likely that you will find any references in the year of the original article's publication. This is because of monthly or quarterly publication patterns, coupled with the time-lags between receipt of manuscripts and their publication. In some fields of science where journals are published weekly, however, articles on current topics may be cited soon after they are published.

3. Note the authors and the abbreviated details of the journals in which the article has been cited.
4. If they are not obvious from the abbreviations, look up the full names of the journals in the list of journals indexed.
5. Search the catalog by title to see whether the library holds these journals and note their call numbers.

A typical citation entry is shown in Figure 17–2. Let's work through this as an example. Assume you have the article by BCM Potts, from the 1992 issue of the *Journal of Natural Products* (Volume 55, page 1701), and you want to know who has cited it. Two people have: DJ Faulkner in *Natural Product Review*, volume 11, 1994, page 355 (the "R" indicates this is a review article) and KB Glaser in *Bioorganic Medicine*, volume 4, 1994, page 1873. Interestingly, Faulkner has also cited two other articles by Potts: in the *Journal of Organic Chemistry*, volume 57, 1992, and the *Journal of the American Chemical Society*, volume 114, 1992.

One word of caution: Authors cite other authors for a variety of reasons. The reason you are hoping for is that the citing author is writing on the same topic as the cited author. But authors sometimes cite other authors to fill their own reference lists with important names or to quote their friends. Unfortunately, sometimes citation leads result in dead ends.

CURRENT AWARENESS

There is a substantial gap between the time a library receives an issue of a journal and the time it receives an index that includes that issue of the journal, even for indexes published on a monthly basis. Two resources address this problem.

Current Contents is published each week by the Institute for Scientific Information and provides bibliographic infor-

Figure 17-2 A typical entry from *Science Citation Index*.

```
POTTS B
  90 TECHNIQUES HIV RES
    HARRICH D          J VIROLOGY           68   5899   94

POTTS BCM
  91 J AM CHEM SOC          113  6321
    VARNEY MD              J MED CHEM        37   2274   94
  92 J NAT PRODUCTS          55  1701
    FAULKNER DJ            NAT PROD R        11    355   94   R
    GLASER KB             BIOORG MED          4   1873   94
  92 J ORG CHEM        57  2965
    FAULKNER DJ            NAT PROD R        11    355   94   R
  92 J AM CHEM SOC          114  5093
    FAULKNER DJ            NAT PROD R        11    355   94   R
    GLASER KB             BIOORG MED          4   1873   94

POTTS BD
  84 CLIN CHEM         30  1374
    SOLANS A              J CHROMAT B       658    380   94   N
  92 J LIQ CHROMATOGR        15   665
    GILAR M               CHEM LISTY         88    514   94   R

POTTS BJ
  89 J VIROL METHODS         26   119
    BOLIN SR              J VIROL MET        48    211   94
  90 TECHNIQUES HIV RES          p103
    PALACIO J             RES VIROL        145    155   94
  90 VIROLOGY          175   465
    CESBRON JY            CR AC S III       317    669   94
    CROWE SM             J LEUK BIOL         56    318   94
    KESSON AM                "             56    241   94
```

Potts article cited

Sources citing Potts article

Other Potts articles cited by Faulkner

mation on articles, reviews, letters, notes, and editorials in more than 8,000 of the world's most important journals. *Current Contents* is indexed by author and title keyword, and abstracts are available for most of the articles. It is published separately by seven broad disciplines (for example: life sciences, social and behavioral sciences, arts and humanities), and is also available on CD-ROM and online.

UnCover is a current awareness service offered by the Colorado Alliance of Research Libraries (CARL) through the Internet (uncweb.carl.org). The *UnCover* database is updated daily and includes about 18,000 journals and 9 million articles. The list of journal titles can be searched by keyword, and the database of articles can be searched by author and keyword. UnCover *Reveal* is a subscription e-mail alert service that delivers the table of contents from requested journals as soon as they are received.

Both *Current Contents* and *UnCover* provide *document delivery* (access to a hard copy of the full text of an article) for a fee, although your library may pay the fee rather than charge users. Check with a reference librarian. Alternatively, you can request articles in journals not held by your library through its interlibrary loan service (see Chapter 20).

NEWSPAPER INDEXES

There are a number of newspaper indexes available, many with full-text retrieval on CD-ROM or online. Note that some may include only selected articles—those over a certain length, with individual bylines, or in particular sections of the newspaper. If you are having trouble locating what you want, check the introduction or accompanying documentation to be sure that this type of material has been included.

Some newspaper indexes may use slightly different conventions for the data elements of date and pagination than do journal indexes. For example, "Jl 13, 24: 3" may refer to the date, page, and column rather than the date, volume, and page.

NewsBank Library is a current-awareness service that provides an index to a microfilm set of more than 100 U.S. newspapers, with separate services for *Review of the Arts* and *Names in the News.* It is the easiest way to locate regional news if your library does not carry newspapers from other states. With monthly, quarterly, and annual cumulations, *NewsBank* focuses on socio-economic, political, and international information from a regional perspective.

NewsBank also publishes on CD-ROM: *NewsSource* is a current awareness service updated five times a year, and the *NewsFile Collection,* with articles from more than 500 news sources, is published annually. It is a good source for "heartland America" viewpoints.

The *National Newspaper Index* is a database covering five major U.S. newspapers: the *New York Times, Los Angeles Times, Wall Street Journal, Washington Post,* and *Christian Science Monitor. Ethnic Newswatch* is another full-text CD-ROM database covering about 200 minority press publications. Native-American, African-American, and Jewish communities are only a few of the publications represented.

Many newspapers and news magazines, some only by paid subscription, are available in full text on the Internet. These include the *New York Times, Wall Street Journal,* and publications from Time Life Inc. Use the Internet guides in Figure 21–1 or the search engines in Figure 21–3 to locate addresses for these and other current news publications.

OTHER TYPES OF INDEXES

Other types of indexes that are extremely useful include those to biographies, book reviews, and media reviews. They are described in more detail below. In addition, there are indexes to a range of literary genres, including poetry, short stories, plays, myths and legends, songs, speeches, and essays. Literary handbooks, described in Chapter 7, supplement these indexes.

The forerunner of the biographical index is the bio-bibliographical *Pinakes*, or *Tables of Persons Eminent in Every Branch of Learning*. It was compiled by Callimachus in the Alexandrian Library between 280 and 250 B.C. Best known today is *Biography Index*, published by the H.W. Wilson Company. It includes articles from periodicals and collective biographies, and provides access by name and occupation.

Two major indexes list where book reviews can be found. They are *Book Review Index* and *Book Review Digest*. To use such sources, you need to look up the author and title of the book in which you are interested, starting with the volume for the year the book was published and continuing for the next few years. Entries list the journal, volume, date, and pages where the review can be found. You then need to use the library's catalog by title to locate the journal.

Book Review Digest entries also include the name of the reviewer, number of words, and short excerpts from the reviews. Depending on your purpose, it may save you from having to locate the original review. *Book Review Index* covers a wider range of books and reviewing journals, but gives only the citation.

The *Readers' Guide to Periodical Literature* indexes film reviews alphabetically by film title under the general heading "Motion picture reviews—Single works." There are also numerous guides to film and video reviews, many of which are available in paperback. Two of the best known are by Leonard Maltin and Pauline Kael.

The Microsoft CD-ROM *Cinemania* reviews 19,000 films and includes 100 audio clips of movie theme songs and 20 full-motion video clips. *CineMedia* is the largest Internet-based film and media directory, with links to more than 25,000 resources online. It is located at afi.cinemedia.org/welcomes/you.html.

There are also guides and indexes to reviews for a range of other information packages, including sound recordings, software, and CD-ROMs. Ask a reference librarian if you need one of these.

DECIDING WHICH FINDING AIDS TO USE

How do you know which of the many indexes and abstracting journals to use for your research query? The parameters for selecting reference works, explained in Chapter 9, apply here. Finding an index or abstracting journal in a library is also very similar to finding a reference work. There are basically three methods.

First, you can use the library catalog by subject. Look up the headings "Subject—Indexes" or "Subject—Abstracts" (for example: "History—Indexes" or "Psychology—Abstracts"). For general indexes, try "Periodicals—Indexes." You should be aware, however, that many of these indexes cover very broad disciplines, so you need to look for the discipline into which your topic falls. If, for example, you are writing a paper on the jaguar motif in Mayan sculpture, you need to see what indexes are available in art or possibly archeology.

Second, you can look up this broad discipline in the library's catalog to determine its classification number. Then browse the shelves in the reference collection under this number.

Third, you can use one of the sources listed in Figure 9–2 to find the names of indexes for the discipline and then search for them in the library catalog by title. If none of these methods succeeds, or if you prefer to take a short cut, ask a reference librarian.

18

Using Bibliographies

In this book, the term "bibliography" has two different meanings: the list of references you append to your essay, and a published list of bibliographic descriptions that can help you discover the existence or determine the identity of information sources. This latter type of bibliography differs from an index in that it often deals with information packages as a whole, rather than their discrete parts.

When might you need to use a bibliography? If you have used the library catalog and found very little about your research topic, a bibliography will show how much has been published on the topic. It may be that very little is available; or alternatively, that a lot has been published, but little is held by the library. This is a sign that the collection you are using is inappropriate, and you need to try elsewhere.

You may have incomplete or inaccurate bibliographic descriptions of information sources likely to be of value and want to verify the details before you start searching for them. Or you may want to find out what has been published most recently on your topic. If you have a reasonable amount of time before your essay or project is due, you could ask your library to order these new information sources.

The headings and data elements in bibliography entries are very similar to those found in library catalogs, minus the call number. Additional data elements may include price, and either an abstract or an annotation.

In order to use bibliographies most effectively, you should analyze them according to the four essential features that apply to all reference works, as discussed in Chapter 2. In choosing among them, you should base your selection on the twelve parameters outlined in Chapter 9.

SUBJECT BIBLIOGRAPHIES, ANNUAL REVIEWS, AND GUIDES TO THE LITERATURE

We have stressed how useful a list of references can be in an encyclopedia or journal article that covers the topic you are researching. Think how very useful it would be to find a whole pamphlet, book, or CD-ROM listing references on the topic. There are such sources, called *subject bibliographies*, which are compiled by experts in the field or librarians familiar with the literature.

Sometimes their scope is wider than the topic you are dealing with. Their contents are often subdivided into narrower topics, however, and one may match yours. A bibliography on organic gardening, for example, may have a section on companion planting, which may be your interest.

Annual reviews, as their name implies, review the literature or current research on different topics. They go by titles starting with "Advances in . . . ," "The Year's Work in . . . ," "Developments in . . . ," and the like. They discuss and sometimes evaluate the contents of relevant research articles. The usefulness of annual reviews is obvious, if you are lucky enough to find one that reviews your research topic.

Guides to the literature are a special type of subject bibliography. They usually cover one discipline, such as chemistry or psychology, and list and discuss the most important reference works, indexes, abstracting journals, bibliographies, books, and journals. They do for the discipline what this book tries to do for information searching in general.

Some libraries provide their own guides to the literature

of a subject field or to their special collections (for example, rare books, government publications, or indexes on CD-ROM). Usually published as pamphlets, they list the major reference works and finding aids, with call numbers, that the library holds. They are an excellent resource for finding your way around a library; keep an eye out for them on display stands or ask at the information desk.

NATIONAL BIBLIOGRAPHIES

Some early bibliographies attempted to be *universal* or *comprehensive*—that is, to cover all publications worldwide. Now they tend to be limited on a national basis, listing information sources published in or about a country. As most national bibliographies started regular publication long after their country's publishing industry began, retrospective national bibliographies have also been compiled in many countries.

The Library of Congress publishes the *National Union Catalog* (*NUC*), which is the most complete record of United States' publications. Since it is also a union catalog, it is described in detail in Chapter 20.

If you have a term paper in history or English and are trying to identify older books, the *National Union Catalog Pre-1956 Imprints* is the most important American retrospective bibliography, containing entries for about 11 million items. Charles Evans' *American Bibliography; A Chronological Dictionary of All Books, Pamphlets and Periodical Publications Printed in the United States of America, from the Genesis of Printing in 1639 Down to and Including the Year 1800* is an important general list of early American publications. The *Dictionary of Books Relating to America, from Its Discovery to the Present Time*, begun by Joseph Sabin in 1868, is another valuable retrospective bibliography.

The United States Government Printing Office (GPO)

supplies extensive catalogs and indexes of its publishing output. This includes Bills, Acts of Congress, Congressional debates, gazettes, and Congressional papers. The GPO also offers centralized publishing, printing, sales, and distribution services to federal government departments and agencies; deposits copies of all its publications at selected libraries; operates government bookstores; and coordinates electronic publishing.

The *British National Bibliography* (*BNB*) covers new works published in the United Kingdom and Ireland. It is arranged by Dewey Decimal Classification, which allows readers familiar with this system to browse through newly-published materials by subject classification. There is an alphabetical author and title index, and an alphabetical subject index to the DDC numbers.

TRADE BIBLIOGRAPHIES

Trade bibliographies are used extensively by the book trade; hence the name. They list the materials published or *in print* (available for purchase from the publisher or a distributor) in a particular country and are usually published annually. Many are also available on microfiche, CD-ROM, or online. As would be expected, one of the important data elements in each entry is the price.

Books in Print lists nearly 1.5 million entries for books published in the United States. There are two main lists of entries: by author/title and by subject. Separate volumes cover children's books, paperbound books, publishers and distributors in the United States, forthcoming books and series, and books out-of-print. The *Books in Print* database is also available on CD-ROM and through many online vendors.

Whitaker's Books in Print (formerly *British Books in Print*) covers United Kingdom publications and worldwide

English-language publications available from sole U.K. agents. It contains over 830,000 titles from 34,000 publishers. There is only one list of entries, but it includes headings for author, title, and keywords from the title in their permuted form; the latter acts as a subject approach to the contents. *Whitaker's BookBank* on CD-ROM and *Whitaker's Books in Print—on Microfiche* are updated monthly.

Cumulative Book Index (CBI), published by the H.W. Wilson Company, contains more than 750,000 entries for books published worldwide in the English language. Author, title, and subject access is in one alphabetical list of entries. *CBI* is also available in CD-ROM and online.

BIBLIOGRAPHIES BY INFORMATION PACKAGE

Even though the prefix "biblio" comes from the Greek word meaning book, today's bibliographies are not limited to books. Indeed, the concept of bibliography predates the Greeks; it is attributed to the Babylonians, who devised rudimentary catalogs for their cuneiform tablets.

Bibliographies of periodicals contain entries for journals and newspapers as a whole, not their discrete parts. *Ulrich's International Periodicals Directory* lists more than 150,000 periodicals currently published throughout the world. Among the many data elements given in the bibliographic descriptions are the abstracting and indexing services that cover the periodicals, the commercial services that provide copies of the periodical articles for a fee, and the URLs for periodicals available on the Internet (see Chapter 21). The *Serials Directory* is a worldwide listing of over 160,000 magazines, journals, and newspapers. It has an alphabetical subject arrangement and lists both Library of Congress and Dewey Decimal Classification numbers for each serial (see Chapter 16).

Bibliographies concentrate on other types of information

packages as well. For example, *Bowker's Complete Video Directory* lists the availability of both entertainment and educational video recordings. There are also bibliographies of conference proceedings, pamphlets, paperbacks, films, microforms, musical scores, CD-ROMs, online databases, and so on. Some even have special names, such as *discographies* for sound recordings and *cartobibliographies* for maps. Still others concentrate on forthcoming publications, reprints, or translations.

As a rule of thumb, if a type of information package exists, some bibliography will cover it, although not necessarily comprehensively.

LEGAL BIBLIOGRAPHY

There are numerous problems in locating information in the legal field. Not only is the law constantly growing and changing, but it comprises hundreds of statutes and regulations and thousands of cases in each jurisdiction. For the federal and each of the state governments, there are indexes and tables that provide access to acts, statutes, and regulations. However, because of amendments and repeals, searches can be quite complex.

Although case law is better indexed than statute law, the names of the cases do not reveal their contents—only the parties to the case. Important cases—either because they establish new legal principles, or because they are from appellate courts (such as the U.S. Supreme Court) and therefore binding on lower courts—are published in law reports.

Citation of cases is complex, but a full citation usually includes the name of the case italicized or underlined, the year of the decision in parentheses, and the volume number, abbreviated title, and first page of the law report series in which it is published. For example, you may be writing a paper identifying major events that led to racial desegregation in schools, and need to refer to the Supreme Court's *Brown vs. Education* decision, which you have seen cited as 347 US 483 (1954). To find it, you must first determine what the abbreviation ("US") stands for—in this case, *United States Reports*. You can then look for this title in the library catalog to find the call number. The case should be in volume 347, starting on page 483.

The *Legal Resource Index* covers over 800 of the major English-language legal publications, including law reviews, law publications, bar association journals, and legal newspapers. The *Index to Legal Periodicals* is an H. W. Wilson publication that indexes legal journals and provides a subject and author index, a book review index, and a table of cases.

The Library of Congress's *Thomas* site (thomas.loc.gov) provides national legislative information on the Internet. There are links to bills in the current Congress, legislation from previous Congresses, the *Congressional Record*, committee reports, directories, and more. *Thomas* takes its name and inspiration from President Thomas Jefferson.

CALR (Computer Assisted Legal Research) has dramatically altered the way legal research is performed. The wide range of resources available through the LEXIS-NEXIS and other legal databases (see Chapter 19) makes it much easier for students, lawyers, and the public to access legal information.

LOCATING AND USING BIBLIOGRAPHIES

How do you locate bibliographies in a library? Although the subject heading "Bibliography" is used in the catalog, bibliographies themselves are not listed. Only information sources *about* bibliographies, such as works on their history or how to compile them, are found there.

To find bibliographies on a particular topic, try looking in the catalog by subject under "Subject—Bibliography" (for example, "Medicine—Bibliography"). Although you may wish to try first under your research topic when looking for bibliographies, you are more likely to find them under a broader heading.

You can locate national and trade bibliographies in the catalog under the subject heading "Name of country—Imprints" or "Name of country—Imprints—Bibliography" (for example, "Japan—Imprints"). You can also locate them in the title catalog under their names. Many, however, are kept in special places in the reference collection because of their continuous use or their large number of volumes. Some are available on microfiche or CD-ROM. It may be easier to ask at the reference desk for their locations.

Bibliographies by information package can be found in the subject catalog under "Type of information package—Catalogs" (for example, "Motion pictures—Catalogs"). Check with your library, as some publish special lists of these.

To find out what bibliographies exist on a topic, you can use a bibliography of bibliographies. The most current is *Bibliographic Index*, published three times yearly by the H.W. Wilson Company. It includes bibliographies that contain 50 or more citations, published separately or appearing as parts of books, pamphlets, or periodicals.

Finding information sources using *Bibliographic Index* is a four-step procedure. You must use:

1. *Bibliographic Index* to find out what bibliographies exist on your topic
2. the catalog by author or title to see whether your library holds these bibliographies
3. the bibliographies to find out what information sources exist on your topic
4. the catalog again by author or title to see whether your library holds these information sources.

19

Using CD-ROM and Online Databases

If you are already familiar with electronic searching of library catalogs, then you'll find that electronic searching of finding aids is very similar. Finding aids on CD-ROMs or online are called *bibliographic databases*, and like catalogs (see Chapter 15), they contain records made up of data elements located in identifiable fields. They cover incredibly diverse subjects—career placement, folklore, pesticides, and wine making, to name just a few.

Many CD-ROM and online databases were once, or still are, published as printed indexes, abstracting journals, or bibliographies. A particular database may be accessible through several CD-ROMs and online system vendors. For example, the National Library of Medicine's MEDLINE database and specialist subsets of it are available on 70 different CD-ROMs produced by numerous companies. MEDLINE is also available online through about 20 different vendors (Braun, 1998, vol. 1: 384; vol. 2: 1145).

After you have carried out a CD-ROM or online search, you are often in the same position as having carried out a manual search: you still have only bibliographic records and not the information itself. You must then determine the library collection most likely to hold the information sources cited and use the library's catalog to find where they are placed on the shelves. Alternatively, some online vendors provide copies of information sources for a fee; check your library's policy to see whether this charge is paid by the library or the user.

CD-ROM AND ONLINE DATABASES

CD-ROMs in Print lists more than 15,500 CD-ROM titles on the market from more than 4,200 producers (Suchowski, 1998: vi). The *Gale Directory of Databases* lists more than 3,900 bibliographic, patent/trademark, full-text, directory, and dictionary databases on CD-ROM (Braun, 1998, vol. 2: x). This compares with fewer than 50 in 1987 (Finlay, 1993: viii).

Many of these same databases, as well as others not found on CD-ROM, are available online. Worldwide, about 5,600 bibliographic, full-text, numeric, and image databases are available online, in some cases through several different vendors (Braun, 1998: x). The number of online searches per year carried out through the major U.S. vendors has grown significantly—from one million in 1975 to nearly 80 million in 1996 (Williams, 1998: xxi).

Many reference works are also available on CD-ROM or online (several were mentioned in Chapters 3 to 8), as are trade bibliographies (discussed in Chapter 18). Among the best known publishers of CD-ROM and online reference works and databases are the H.W. Wilson Company, Knight-Ridder Information Inc. (formerly Dialog), SilverPlatter Information Inc., Ovid Technologies, and Reed Elsevier.

ERIC and *Dissertation Abstracts*

Two databases available both on CD-ROM and online deserve special mention because of their usefulness. Teacher-education students will find *ERIC* of great value, and graduate students—or for that matter, any students who are writing major papers—will find *Dissertation Abstracts* worth searching.

The Educational Resources Information Center (ERIC) was established by the United States Office of Education in the mid-1960s. Its purpose was to collect, index, and make available on microfiche all unpublished, non-copyright materials of value in education. You can search the *ERIC* database using sophisticated searching strategies to pinpoint your topic. ERIC also produces printed abstracts to these materials (*Resources in Education*) and to educational journal articles (*Current Index to Journals in Education*).

Dissertation Abstracts International, which is published by UMI, provides lengthy summaries of doctoral theses from more than 1,000 universities worldwide. The database contains entries for more than one million theses and adds about 42,000 entries each year. Theses are valuable because they review related literature in detail before describing the research undertaken. Sometimes the abstract itself is enough to supply the information you need. If you identify a thesis that you think is relevant but your library does not hold it, it can be ordered in microform or various paper formats from UMI (www.umi.com).

FULL-TEXT DATABASES

Some CD-ROM and online databases contain not only bibliographic records, but the complete text of information sources as well. These are called *full-text databases*. Examples include newspaper articles (see Chapter 17), standards, legislation, and a wide range of literature. Some directories that list the availability of full-text materials on CD-ROM or online are included in Figure 19–1.

The LEXIS/NEXIS databases provide the full texts of reported and unreported opinions of state and federal courts; statutes; regulatory documents; looseleaf services; wire, television, and radio news transcripts; and many newspapers. WESTLAW also offers full-text legal information.

English Poetry provides access on CD-ROM to the full

Figure 19–1 Directories listing CD-ROMs and online databases available worldwide.

Bjorner, Susanne, ed. 1995. *Newspapers Online: A Guide to Searching Daily Newspapers Whose Articles Are Online in Full Text.* 3rd ed. Needham Heights, Massachusetts: BiblioData.

Braun, Erin E., ed. 1998. *Gale Directory of Databases.* 2 vols. Detroit: Gale Research.

DataBase Directory. 1995. White Plains, New York: Knowledge Industry Publications.

Hogan, Kathleen M. and James H. Shelton, eds. 1995. *CD-ROM Finder.* 6th ed. Medford, New Jersey: Learned Information.

Multimedia Year Book and CD-ROM Directory. 1997. 16th ed. 2 vols. London: TFPL Multimedia.

Niles, Ann, ed. 1995. *CD-ROM Book Index: An International Guide to Full-text Books on CD-ROM.* Medford, New Jersey: Learned Information.

Nobari, Nuchine, ed. 1998. *Books and Periodicals Online, A Directory of Online Publications.* Washington, D.C.: Library Technology Alliance.

Orenstein, Ruth M. 1998. *BiblioData Fulltext Sources Online* 10, no. 2 (July). Needham, Massachusetts: BiblioData.

Suchowski, Amy R., ed. 1998. *CD-ROMs in Print.* 12th ed. Detroit: Gale Research.

---

text of English poetry from A.D. 600 to 1900 for poets listed in the *New Cambridge Bibliography of English Literature.* Similarly, *English Prose Drama* contains more than 1,800 plays by 400 authors from the Renaissance to 1900. You can use these discs simply to locate and read a work, or alternatively, to carry out complex stylistic and linguistic analyses.

Library of the Future is a CD-ROM that includes the complete text and illustrations of more than 3,500 works from 800 B.C. to the present. Coverage includes classical and modern literature; religious texts; and historical, political, and scientific works. You can search the disc by title, author, word, age, era or century, country, subject category, and illustration. Several video clips are also included.

Project Gutenberg (promo.net/pg) is a valuable Internet resource containing nearly 2,000 non-copyrighted books and historical documents,. It can be searched by author, title, subject, language, and Library of Congress classification. Files can be downloaded by FTP (see Chapter 21).

NUMERIC AND IMAGE DATABASES

Numeric databases provide information in numerical form either at a fixed date or over time. They include census figures (see Chapter 7), stock market or other financial data, meteorological and environmental data, opinion polls, and other statistical information.

Image databases have graphic representations as a key data element in their records. These images may include chemical or molecular structures and properties, trademarks, photographs, art reproductions, or *clip art* (illustrations that can be used without copyright), and so on.

For example, the Library of Congress *American Memory* collections on the Internet (memory.loc.gov) provide images as diverse as Civil War photographs, baseball cards, dance instruction manuals, portraits of presidents and first ladies, railroad maps, "Votes for Women" suffrage pictures, the Spanish-American war in motion pictures, panoramic photographs from 1851 to 1991—and much more.

COMPARING ELECTRONIC AND MANUAL SEARCHES

What advantages do CD-ROM and online searches have over manual searches of printed finding aids? In general, their bibliographic records are more detailed and their searching options are more sophisticated. In particular:

- You can search for any word or phrase as an access term—not just the limited number of headings selected by an indexer—which is a very powerful tool for pinpointing information.
- You can combine access terms using the logical operators AND, OR, and NOT (see Chapter 10), which can help you clearly define the information you are looking for and eliminate unwanted material.
- You can search across the full bibliographic record or limit your search to designated fields. The title, abstract, and subject descriptor fields are most useful in this respect.
- You can narrow a search that has retrieved too many items by using the full range of data elements—for example, choosing to look at those that were published in a particular journal, after a certain date, or only in English.
- You get results much more quickly. Not only is the search faster and more targeted, but if your computer is connected to a printer, you can print out the bibliographic records on the spot. This saves having to tediously copy down details. Alternatively, you may be able to store the results on a floppy disk to manipulate later.
- Assuming a topic is of continuing interest (if you are writing a thesis, for example), you can arrange with your library to get an automatic search of your topic against the most recent portion of the database every time it is updated (usually monthly or quarterly).

- Many databases, especially those available online, are more up-to-date than their printed counterparts. Some databases are not available in printed versions at all.

There are also disadvantages to electronic searching:

- You can easily retrieve irrelevant information with an electronic search—that is, sources that may technically "match" the access terms, but that are not really about the topic. These are called *noise* or *false drops*. For example, a search on "solar ponds," which combines the terms "solar" and "ponds," may lead to an article on solar cars—retrieved because it was published in Moonee Ponds, Australia!
- The computer, unlike a human brain, is unforgiving with respect to spelling. If you misspell a word, the computer will not find it—whereas browsing in a printed index you might. Likewise, data entered into the computer can be misspelled—which means you are unlikely to find the information unless you make the same mistake. To my amazement I recently retrieved database entries when I entered "scupture" instead of "sculpture" and "Henduras" instead of "Honduras," because the input data had been equally erroneous!
- Some topics are inappropriate for database searching. Those that are very broad, such as computers in libraries or the history of science, would retrieve way too much material to be useful.
- Retrospective searching may be limited, as many computer databases generally go no further back than the mid-1960s. To gather information before this, you would need to consult printed finding aids as well.
- When using a computer, you miss the opportunity to skim or browse information located on nearby pages. The informal scanning that goes on when you are searching for your topic can often serendipitously turn up useful information.

CARRYING OUT AN ELECTRONIC SEARCH

In many ways, CD-ROM and online searching is similar to using a library catalog, so you should be able to undertake a simple search without assistance. If your search is more complex, however, or you would like to find out some of the special features of CD-ROM or online databases, you may find it helpful to take a short training course, if your library offers one.

Your library catalog may be on a campus network that also provides access to CD-ROMs and online databases, and you may be able to search all three from the same computer. If this is the case, starting a CD-ROM or online search may be similar to starting a catalog search.

Regardless of your library's network setup, there will probably be some separate CD-ROM stations available to search additional resources, and you will need to note carefully the varied search instructions for each one. You may also have to schedule time to use a CD-ROM drive, if the facilities are busy.

Although specific procedures vary for searching different CD-ROMs and online databases, they follow the same general pattern. Before starting, you should review your topic and list of possible search terms (see Chapter 10), then undertake the steps below. They are listed briefly and then explained in greater detail:

1. Select the database.
2. Choose which data elements and fields to search in the bibliographic record.
3. Combine the search terms using logical operators or proximity connectors.
4. View the results and modify your search to expand or limit it.

Selecting the Database

Often, a good place to start is the Online Computer Library Center (OCLC) *FirstSearch* service (see also Chapter 20). *FirstSearch* contains over 70 databases, including articles from 35,000 journals, more than one million full-text documents delivered on screen or by e-mail, a range of reference works, and links to library collections worldwide through *WorldCat*. *FirstSearch* uses the same search strategy for all its databases, which makes it easy to use. You can choose one or more databases from a subject area list, and then use either a basic (subject keyword) or more advanced search.

Whether you are using *FirstSearch* or other databases, the parameters for selecting among them are similar to the parameters for selecting among reference works (see Chapter 9). You need to decide which databases, based on their geographical coverage, languages, dates of coverage, discipline, scope, audience, and so forth, are most relevant to your topic. There are several ways you can do this:

- The library may have printed or online guides that describe the databases available.
- Many databases have opening screens that indicate their contents.
- Some systems have online indexes that indicate how many times a search term is used in each database, as an aid in deciding which one is best.
- Some of the directories in Figure 19–1 provide descriptions of CD-ROM and online databases, with access through a subject index.
- Best of all, a reference librarian can tell you the databases to which the library has access, help you to decide which one is most appropriate for your topic, and assist you in the search.

For the database you select, check the HELP screens and

note any special searching strategies. For example, some databases are divided into five-year or ten-year time periods for searching purposes, with each period treated as a separate database. Others enable you to search for or limit your topic in special ways. For example, some legal databases permit you to search by case or statute number. PsycINFO (the online version of *Psychological Abstracts*) and Health-STAR permit you to limit your search topic by age group.

Choosing the Data Elements and Fields

You can search databases by author or title, using the author or title fields, to find articles by an author whom you know writes on your topic or to verify details of articles that are incorrectly cited. Most searching is by subject, however, so databases offer a variety of options to suit this type of search. These may include searches by:

- *Keywords* (see below), which are all the substantive words in a bibliographic record that can be used to access the information source.
- *Descriptors* (see below), which are standardized terms assigned to a bibliographic record to describe the information source, regardless of the terms used by the author. They are analogous to the Library of Congress subject headings in library catalogs.
- *Identifiers*, which indicate persons, organizations, time periods, geographic areas, species, and so on, related to an information source, although they do not comprise the subject per se. Typical identifiers might include "Cretaceous period," "Lake Baikal," "*Australopithecus robustus*," or "Federal Trade Commission." During a search, identifiers can be combined with other types of search terms to pinpoint topics by particular time, place, or affiliation.
- *Discipline*, which indicates a broad subject field, such as "Heritage," "Geology," or "Zoology." During a

search, it can be combined with other search terms to cover a topic from a particular perspective.

You may also have the option of choosing which fields to search within the bibliographic record—for example, author, article title, journal or book title, subject descriptor, abstract, or full record. In general, the more fields you search, the more items you are likely to retrieve—and the more items that are likely to be irrelevant. This relationship is explained in more detail later in the chapter. If your initial search retrieves too many items, you may also have the option at this stage of selecting additional fields, such as date, publisher, or place of publication, by which to limit your search.

KEYWORD SEARCHING

If you have never carried out a CD-ROM or online search before, you may want to begin with keyword searching. It is the broadest kind of search and is most useful when you do not know the correct descriptors for your topic or your topic is not well defined by a descriptor.

Decide which search terms to use, chosen from among those you listed in the beginning steps of your search strategy (see Chapter 10). If you have already found one or two articles central to your topic, they should be a good guide to the terminology.

You may have the option of using *truncation* or *wildcards* to extend a search term by retrieving all terms that start with a given combination of letters. In some systems, for example, "librar#" would retrieve items with access terms starting with the first six letters listed, including "library," "libraries," "librarian," "librarians," and "librarianship." The HELP screens for your database should tell you if the number symbol (#), or alternatively, an asterisk, question mark, dollar sign, or some other symbol, is used.

Sometimes you can put a number after the wildcard symbol to indicate the number of characters that may follow the root word. For example, "geo$5" would retrieve "geodesic," "geologic," and "geometry," but not "geode," "geometric," or "geostationary."

The concept of stop words, which was discussed in connection with KWIC indexes in Chapter 17, is also relevant to keyword searches. Articles ("a", "an," and "the"), conjunctions ("and," "but," "so," "because," and so on), and prepositions ("of," "for," "to," "with," and so on) are eliminated as search terms, because they are so common that they take up too much computer time in processing. In some systems, common substantive words from titles such as "introduction" or "journal" are also eliminated.

DESCRIPTOR SEARCHING

Searching using descriptors is preferable if your topic is fairly clearly defined. This type of search will retrieve all items about a topic regardless of the terminology used by the author. It also narrows a search by retrieving only items that cover the topic in depth.

You can locate the correct descriptors for your research topic by scanning the subject "browse" list. This list shows only the terms used as headings, so if the term you're searching for isn't there, you'll have to think up synonymous or perhaps broader terms to look under.

Some databases also have a printed *thesaurus* of terms used in the database. (Do not confuse this meaning of the word "thesaurus" with the reference books discussed in Chapter 6.) The thesaurus does for a database what the *Library of Congress Subject Headings* does for library collections: it provides a standardized list of subject access terms, with "see" references from the terms not used. Some thesauruses also show the terms in a hierarchical structure, similar to a classification scheme. Two thesauruses that you may find useful are the *Thesaurus of ERIC Descriptors* published by the Educational Resources Information Center and the

Thesaurus of Psychological Index Terms published by the American Psychological Association.

Combining Search Terms

The same logical operators (AND, OR, and NOT) that you used to define your topic (see Chapter 10) can also be used to carry out your search. You need to decide which ones to use and the order in which to use them. You may want to consider in advance alternative strategies for either narrowing or expanding your search, depending on the initial results.

For example, "hurricanes AND Mississippi" will narrow your search about hurricanes to those in one state, while "skiing NOT water" will eliminate items covering water skiing, while leaving those about downhill and cross-country skiing. Alternatively, "workers OR laborers" will expand a search by retrieving items containing one or the other or both of these terms.

You may also have the option of specifying particular distances between the keywords you select—for example, adjacent to each other, within the same sentence, or within the same field. Some databases automatically assume *adjacency* (that the keywords are immediately next to each other, with no other words intervening), while others do not. This means that if you use a phrase such as "mountain rescue" and your database does not recognize adjacency, you may also pick up articles such as "The Rescue of Wild Life in the Olympic Mountain Region."

In some databases, the word connectors NEAR, SAME, and WITH are used to denote the relative distance, or *proximity*, although the meaning of these terms may change from database to database. The HELP screen should tell you which connectors are used and what they mean.

For example, in one database "wine WITH California" might mean that the search terms must occur in the same sentence before they will be retrieved, while "steroid SAME athlete" might require that they occur in the same field or paragraph. "Rhythm NEAR blues" could mean that the first term must be next to the second term, but in any order.

Viewing Results and Modifying Searches

Once you enter a search statement, you are given the *set number* (starting with #1) and *postings* (the number of occurrences of the search term) for each of the terms individually and in combination. Although search terms may have numerous postings individually, when a series of logical operators or proximity connectors is used with them, the final result may be only a few or no postings.

To modify your search, you can combine existing sets with new search terms or with each other. Continue entering search statements, viewing results, and modifying your search until you have found as many items as you need or you are satisfied that you have found all the relevant items. You may need to identify two or three times the number of information sources you actually need, as not all of them will be available on the shelves or even in your library.

A hypothetical search is shown in the next section, followed by strategies for modifying your search depending on the initial results.

A HYPOTHETICAL SEARCH

Each CD-ROM disc or online service has particular *protocols*, or sets of instructions as to how a search can be carried out. These vary from one product or vendor to another. Just as with using library catalogs, you may have to experiment a bit to determine how each one works. The best way to get a general idea is by an example. Suppose you have to write a paper on "Dinosaurs and extinction: What we know from the fossil record." You may decide to begin with a keyword search on dinosaur fossils, and your first search statement might be:

KEYWORDS:	dinosaur$ AND fossil$

In this case, you will retrieve all the items that include the terms "dinosaur" and "fossil," "dinosaur" and "fossils," "dinosaurs" and "fossil," and "dinosaurs" and "fossils." You haven't indicated any particular field or proximity, so each of the search terms could appear anywhere in the bibliographic record. The results might be:

Set number	Postings	Search term
#1	1,799	dinosaur$
#2	3,648	fossil$
#3	908	dinosaur$ AND fossil$

Nine hundred articles is way more than you want. To continue to narrow your search, you can use the numbered sets that have resulted from the search statement. To add the third concept of extinction to your search, the next search statement might be:

KEYWORDS:	#3 AND extinction

with the following results:

#4	254	extinction
#5	86	#3 AND extinction

With this combination, you have retrieved 86 bibliographic records—still too many. You might now want to use one or more data elements, such as country of publication, date, or language, to limit your search. This might result in a final set of, say, 23 items.

Even then, you might find that some of the titles you retrieved will not be central to your topic—for example, "Presenting Paleontology to Students from Grades 9 to 12," which discusses how teachers can interest students in paleontology by using fossil samples in the classroom and encouraging students to do library research about why dinosaurs became extinct. So perhaps 18 of the records retrieved will be useful.

RECALL AND PRECISION

There are two concepts in database searching—recall and precision—that are helpful in explaining how effectively you are carrying out a search. They can be expressed as simple formulas:

Recall = n/c   where n equals the number of relevant information sources you retrieve and c equals the total number of relevant information sources in the collection—that is, the number you ought to have retrieved if your search was "perfect."

Precision = n/t   where n equals the number of relevant information resources you retrieve and t equals the total number of information resources you retrieve.

Obviously you can't calculate your recall for a search, as you would never know how many relevant information sources you never found! You can get a rough idea of your precision, however, by gauging how many of the items you retrieved are actually useful. In the hypothetical example above, you retrieved 23 articles, of which 18 were relevant, for a precision ratio of 18/23, or about 78 percent.

The reason the concepts of recall and precision are helpful is that, in general, they are inversely related to each other. That is, the higher the recall, the lower the precision; or the lower the recall, the higher the precision. Knowing this can help you to modify your search to obtain better results.

MODIFYING A SEARCH

If you are not finding enough information and want to increase your recall, there are a number of techniques available. You can:

- search additional databases that are not quite as closely related to your subject discipline, but that might still have some relevant items
- expand a concept by adding a range of subsets (for example: "dogs OR dalmatians OR cocker spaniels OR dachshunds OR poodles," and so on)
- truncate terms to add plural or other related word forms ("botan#" to retrieve "botanical," "botanist," "botanists," "botany")
- broaden a concept by using a more general term ("marsupials" rather than "kangaroos")
- reduce the number of concepts you combine in a search ("population AND unemployment" or "migrants AND unemployment," rather than "population AND migrants AND unemployment")
- decrease the required proximity between terms (the terms "personnel" and "management" can appear anywhere within a bibliographic record, rather than adjacent to each other in that order).

In increasing your recall, however, remember that you usually decrease your precision. You will retrieve more records, but a larger proportion of these records may not match your topic as closely, or in some cases, at all.

Alternatively, if you have too much information at your

disposal, you may want to increase your precision. To do this you can:

- search only the most appropriate databases
- narrow the concept (for example: "speleology" rather than "caves")
- add to the number of concepts you combine in a search ("population AND migrants AND unemployment AND urban")
- limit the search to particular fields in the record (say, title and abstract only)
- limit the search to descriptors in the descriptor field, as opposed to keywords used anywhere in the record
- limit the search by other data elements, such as date, language, or country of publication, if they are available.

For example, having searched for "wine WITH California", you may wish to limit your search by the date (1990–), by type of publication (journals), or by language (English only; you don't want articles in Spanish about Baja California). Or, if you are searching for drug abuse among teenagers, you may decide to limit your search to studies designated as dealing with adolescents aged 13 to 17 years.

ONLINE ACCESS

Databases from some online vendors can be accessed through the World Wide Web as well as by subscription. Many universities and colleges now try to use the Web for searching when possible, because subscriptions are expensive.

Indeed, databases on the Web are available to any user with a credit card. If you have Internet access and are willing to pay the costs, you can search using a browser's search strategies (see Chapter 21) rather than the more complicated protocols of the vendor's subscription product.

Occasionally you may need to search a very specialized database, or perhaps you do not have time to undertake an extensive search. You may prefer to use a *mediated* search by a professional searcher in the library and information field. Contact your university or public library, or consult a directory of database searchers, to find someone available locally.

If you decide that you need such assistance, the main points to consider are the following:

- If possible, arrange to sit with the searcher during the search. You are the best judge of which of the search terms are most useful to your topic and which of the bibliographic records retrieved seem the most relevant.
- There is usually a charge for a mediated search—sometimes just for the printout of the results, but sometimes for the connect time and the searcher's time as well. Different vendors have different pricing structures; some may be less expensive than others for accessing the same information. Your college or university library probably has a base fee for students.
- Printouts of the results can be taken offline to save money, which may mean a wait. You should find out the likely costs and delays in advance from the person undertaking the search for you.

20

Union Lists and Inter-library Lending

Not all of the information sources that you identify from a manual or electronic search will be held in the library you are using as home base. In this case, you may want to consult a *union list* or *union catalog* to find the collections in which these sources are held. Union lists do for groups of collections what library catalogs do for individual collections.

Union lists may be in print, microfiche, CD-ROM, or online. Entries consist of a bibliographic record with *holdings symbols*—that is, unique identification codes for each of the libraries that owns an information source. The first part of the code designates the state and the second part designates the library (for example: NYPL is the New York Public Library; CtY is Yale University).

Some union lists also give each library's holdings in more detail. This could include call number and number of copies for books, and call number, opening date, missing issues, and closing date for journals (see Chapter 15).

There are union lists by information packages, subject disciplines, geographic areas, types of libraries, and combinations of these. You might, for example, find a union list of Latin American periodicals in California, or astronomy films and videos held by college and university libraries in Chicago. Union lists available online give the holdings for libraries subscribing to particular cataloging, inter-library lending, or other bibliographic services.

THE *NATIONAL UNION CATALOG* AND OTHER UNION LISTS

The *National Union Catalog* lists information sources—by author, title, and subject—that are published throughout the world and cataloged by the Library of Congress. It also includes the holdings of many other libraries in the United States because of a cooperative cataloging program to which these libraries contribute.

The *National Union Catalog Pre-1956 Imprints* is a cumulative author list and includes holdings from the Library of Congress and more than 700 libraries in the United States and Canada. With about 11 million entries in 754 volumes (including a supplement), it represents the history of book publishing in the United States from its beginning.

This catalog was actually published after the *National Union Catalog, 1952–1957*, which was the first attempt to merge the printed cards of the Library of Congress with the holdings of other libraries. There have been several supplements. The last catalog in book form was published in 1979, and since then it appears in microform. The catalog no longer reports the holdings of the libraries that are members of the Online Computer Library Center (OCLC) Network, the Research Libraries Network (RLN), or the Western Library Network (WLN).

The *Union List of Serials in Libraries of the United States and Canada* includes more than 156,000 serial titles with holdings in 956 cooperating libraries. It is continued by *New Serial Titles* (*NST*), which lists publications after 1950. In 1981 *NST* became a product of the CONSER (CONversion of SERials) project, an online cooperative database of more than 850,000 serial titles.

OCLC, RLN, and WLN

American libraries have developed a strong tradition of cooperation over many years. This has been formalized through the concept of shared cataloging and merging of holdings records.

OCLC began as a network for Ohio libraries and gradually became a nationwide database containing the holdings of a large number of college, university, public, and special libraries. Soon libraries worldwide, including the British Library and the French Bibliotheque Nationale, were adding their holdings to OCLC.

MARC (Machine Readable Cataloging) records, which list the holdings of the Library of Congress, form the base of OCLC. Selected member libraries are also permitted to enter their original cataloging records on MARC. Other member libraries may attach their holdings symbol to records already created by the Library of Congress or member libraries.

OCLC's online union catalog, called *WorldCat*, includes more than 35 million records and is updated daily. It contains books, magazines, sound recordings, maps, films, videotapes, manuscripts, and any other material cataloged by OCLC's member libraries throughout the world. It is accessible to users through the *FirstSearch* service (see Chapter 19).

By using the OCLC interlibrary loan system, subscribers can easily identify which library holds a particular item and order it. To identify these libraries, OCLC publishes the *OCLC Holdings Symbols Directory*.

RLN and WLN are similar to OCLC. They, too, make use of MARC records from the Library of Congress and their member libraries.

ACCESS TO SOURCES IN OTHER LIBRARIES

Once you have discovered the location or locations of an information source in a union list, the next step is a matter of choice. If the source is a book or journal article and it is in a local library, it may be easiest to go to that library and read or photocopy it there. All public and many college, university, and special libraries allow use by the public.

If the information source you want is not available locally, you may wish to ask your library to request it on *interlibrary loan (ILL)*. This is a formal system set up by libraries throughout the United States to facilitate the interchange of material for users who need it. Your library will forward a request to one of the libraries identified as holding it, and that library will provide either a photocopy (for journal articles) or the source itself (for monographs or audiovisual materials).

Libraries may have special ILL rules. They may make requests only when no library in the greater metropolitan area holds an item. Some may require that information sources borrowed through ILL be used on the premises, while others may allow them to be checked out. There is usually no charge to users for interlibrary loan requests.

Ariel is a new software program that is radically changing ILL delivery. Ariel transmits documents by digital scanning from the library holding the material to the library requesting it. Although material can be sent quickly by fax machine, the copy is sometimes not clear. Material stored digitally can be sent very rapidly and is usually of high quality.

Some university library interlibrary loan services are already providing document delivery to desktops. A more likely possibility in the future is that they will send information to an Internet site that can be accessed at a Uniform Resource Locator (URL) by a certain date (see Chapter 21).

Occasionally, no U.S. library will hold an information

source. In this case, an inter-library loan request can be placed overseas. The library used most often for overseas borrowing is the British Library Document Supply Centre, which tries to maintain as comprehensive a collection of journals as possible for just this purpose. In cases of urgency, requests can be telephoned, faxed, or sent by e-mail.

21

The Internet

S o much has been written about the Internet that it is difficult to know where to start. Many of the guide books available are longer than 300 pages. The goal of this chapter is to provide a brief overview of the types of information sources available and the searching procedures needed to locate them. Then it's up to you to explore.

But be warned: First, the Internet is a great time-waster for the unwary. Don't let access to too much information be an excuse for failing your exams! Second, the millions of users worldwide are not uncritical enthusiasts. Some have likened the Internet to grabbing a handful of jelly and watching it ooze out between your fingers. Others have called it as user friendly as Genghis Khan with saddle sores. One expert (Anthes, 1996: 70) said that "the Web is a case study of chaos theory."

So, although it is possible to find your way around by trial and error, it may be best to enroll in an introductory course or ask a friend to show you how it works. If neither of these options is available, borrow or purchase a beginner's guide. Several are given in Figure 21–1, but this list is far from comprehensive. To find additional published guides, try *Smartbooks.com* (smartbooks.com) on the Internet under the categories "Introductory/General guides" and "Directories/ searching".

Figure 21–1 Useful guidebooks and directories to the Internet.

Crowder, David and Rhonda Crowder. 1999. *Teach Yourself the Internet*. Foster City, California: IDG Books Worldwide.

Crumlish, Christian. 1998. *The Internet for Busy People*. 3rd ed. Berkeley, California: Osborne/McGraw-Hill.

Ellsworth, Jill H. 1998. *The Internet Unleashed*. Indianapolis, Indiana: Sams.net Publishing.

Gilster, Paul. 1997. *Digital Literacy*. New York: John Wiley.

Gilster, Paul. 1997. *The Web Navigator*. 4th ed. New York: John Wiley.

Hahn, Harley. 1999. *Harley Hahn's Internet and Web Golden Directory*. Berkeley, California: Osborne/McGraw-Hill.

Levine, John, Carol Baroudi, and Margaret Levine Young. 1999. *The Internet for Dummies*. 6th ed. Foster City, California: IDG Books Worldwide.

McGuire, Mary, Linda Stilborne, Melinda McAdams, and Laurel Hyatt. 1997. *The Internet Handbook for Writers, Researchers, and Journalists*. New York: Guilford Press.

Maxwell, Bruce. 1997. *How to Access the Federal Government on the Internet 1998*. Washington, D.C.: Congressional Quarterly.

Mogge, Dru, ed. 1997. *Directory of Electronic Journals, Newsletters, and Academic Discussion Lists*. 7th ed. Washington, D.C.: Association of Research Libraries.

Teach Yourself the Internet in 24 Hours. 1998. 2nd ed. Indianapolis, Indiana: Sams.net Publishing.

Young, Margaret Levine, et al. 1999. *Internet: The Complete Reference*. Millennium ed. Berkeley, California: Osborne/McGraw-Hill.

Your university library's homepage may link to some of the numerous beginners' guides available on the Internet. If not, you can access several from the Library of Congress Internet site (lcweb.loc.gov/global/internet/training.html). Alternatively, use the *Yahoo!* search engine (yahoo.com) and follow the menu pathway: Computers and Internet → Internet → Information and Documentation → Beginner's guides. (Search engines are explained in more detail later in this chapter.)

If you are uncertain about any Internet terminology, you can consult a number of Internet dictionaries online. These include *NetLingo* (netlingo.com) and the *Free On-Line Dictionary of Computing* (nightflight.com/foldoc).

This book has mentioned only a very few of the millions of Internet sites available, because the Internet is in a constant state of flux and addresses may change without notice. To stay up to date, read current guidebooks or magazines, tap into Internet current awareness services, or just roam around to see what's there.

THE ORIGINS

The Internet evolved from a network set up originally by the U.S. Defense Department in the late 1960s. ARPAnet was an experimental network designed to support military research; it used the *Internet Protocol* (*IP*) to enable data to be transferred among the computers comprising the network. Hence the name, Internet.

In the late 1980s, the National Science Foundation used the IP protocol to set up interconnected networks among the major universities in the United States. These and other interconnected networks—the Internet—continue to grow in number of subscribers and are being upgraded to handle the increase in traffic.

Most colleges and universities now provide student access

to the Internet through the library or the computer center. If these facilities are crowded, however, you may want to consider subscribing from home. There are an increasing number of organizations, known as *Internet Service Providers* (*ISPs*), that offer public access to the Internet for public, private, or commercial users. For example, there are over 50 ISPs in the Seattle area alone.

To check on ISPs in your area, look in the *Yellow Pages* under "Internet Providers." Be sure to ask these services whether they have *Points of Presence* (*POP*), or local phone lines, in your area. Otherwise, you may have to pay long distance charges each time you sign online. Set-up and usage fees may also vary.

To access the Internet from a college computer, you may need to click on an Internet browser icon, select the Internet option from a menu, or type in specific commands. Once connected, you can move from your computer to any other on the network and access whatever resources it provides. This sharing of resources is implemented by two separate types of computer programs: the data-handling software that provides the resources is called the *server*, and the user-interface software that requests the resources is called the *client*.

E-MAIL

You can communicate with someone more quickly by *electronic mail*, or *e-mail*, than by traditional "snail mail" or even fax—although it depends on the recipient logging on to receive the message. To send and receive mail, you are issued a unique address in the form: Personal identifier@ organization.type of user. The address to the right of the @ sign is called the *domain*, which consists of two or more parts separated by periods (usually called dots). For overseas users, there is often an additional last part of the domain that indicates country.

You should recognize the organizations that are universities by their abbreviations (for example,"msu" is Michigan State University; "usc" is the University of Southern California). Types of users include "edu" (educational institutions), "gov" (government), "org" (organizations), and "com" (commercial organizations and businesses).

Most e-mail software provides instructions that can be selected from a menu or input as commands. The most common are to retrieve messages, read messages, send messages, create folders to store the messages you send or receive, store messages, delete messages, add names to an address list, and delete names from an address list.

Depending on the software your computer uses, you may be able to carry out additional tasks. For example, you may be able to transfer messages to e-mail from word processing software, print out or download messages, forward messages to other people, or send messages to a group of people at once.

Eudora and PINE are two publicly available e-mail software packages you may come across. You can also communicate across the Internet using video and voice. Cornell University's video-conferencing program, CU-SeeMe, is free on the Internet. In addition to the software, it requires the availability of a video camera.

USENET GROUPS

The Internet has several million participants involved in more than 20,000 different discussion groups. They are of two types: Usenet newsgroups and electronic mailing lists. Many of the Internet guides in Figure 21–1 contain directories of both types. There are also several directories of discussion groups on the Internet.

Usenet groups are each devoted to a particular topic, and the topics range widely: AIDS treatment, Batman comics, population biology, and quilting, to name just a few. Subscribers to Usenet groups "call in" to read the news and articles that other participants have posted and, if they wish, add their own comments to the issues being discussed.

ELECTRONIC MAILING LISTS

Like Usenet groups, electronic mailing lists concentrate on particular topics. A few at random: KLARINET is about clarinet playing; HuntDog-L, hunting dogs; Arcana, the occult; Grunge-L, grunge rock; Allergy, all types of human allergies, their treatment, and their effect on health and lifestyle; BIBSOFT, software for citations and bibliographies; and COMEDIA, Hispanic classic theater.

If you subscribe to an electronic mailing list, you receive e-mail copies of all news and articles that other subscribers have sent to the central mailing address, and you can forward your own comments to distribute to everyone else on the list as well. The number of messages you receive depends on the number of subscribers to the list and how active they are. If an issue is of current interest, more people will want to have their say. Some lists offer a digest, so that the e-mail messages for the day or week arrive together rather than individually.

The electronic record keeping for mailing lists is handled by programs such as Listserv, Listproc, Mailserv, or Majordomo. The address for subscribing is usually different from the central mailing address for correspondence. For example, to subscribe to a mailing list on Listserv, say DorothyL (an electronic mailing list on mystery literature), you e-mail to: listserv@listserv.kent.edu with the message: "subscribe dorothyl" followed by your first name and surname. When you get tired of being on the list, you send a message to the same address saying: "unsubscribe dorothyl" again followed by your first name and surname. The trick is to store the address in a place where you can find it again when you need it!

ELECTRONIC NEWSLETTERS AND JOURNALS

Publications such as electronic newsletters and journals (or *e-journals*) are some of the most valuable information resources on the Internet. They combine the immediacy of electronic publication with the knowledge of a wide range of experts.

The *Directory of Electronic Journals, Newsletters, and Academic Discussion Lists* has been published by the Association of Research Libraries (ARL), both online and in print, since 1991. In 1997, it listed more than 3,400 electronic journals, newsletters, and magazines, and more than 3,800 academic discussion lists—about 11.5 times the number in 1991. The ARL (arl.org/scomm/edir/index.html) also announces new electronic journals as they become available.

FTP

File Transfer Protocol (*FTP*) sites with their own set of data files are similar to individual libraries with their own set of books—except that rather than "borrowing" a data file, you can download it to your own computer, store it, print it out, change it, or send it to someone else. There are over two million public FTP files, including electronic texts, journals, newsletters, software, and graphics.

To locate an FTP file, you need to know its site name, directory path, and file name. To transfer some types of files, you need to have an account and password. This is not the case, however, for *anonymous FTP*. This facility allows you to copy files that have been purposely set up so that anyone on the Internet can retrieve them. In fact, you can even use anonymous FTP to request several free guides on how to use the Internet!

When accessing an anonymous FTP file, type "anonymous" when asked for a user name and your e-mail address when asked for a password. Once you are connected, you will need to indicate the name of the *sourcefile*—that is, the file you want to transfer to your computer. Often, computer servers that are set up to distribute files have numerous files stored in various directories. Thus, you may have to issue commands to change directories or list the files to find the one you want.

How do you know what files are available at all the anonymous FTP sites? Most of the newer search engines (explained later in this chapter) will take you directly to those files via a subject search. You can also use Archie-server software, which receives lists of all FTP files. But Archie is quickly being superseded by these search engines.

WAIS AND CWIS

The *Wide Area Information Server* (*WAIS*, pronounced 'wayz') is yet another type of Internet information access. WAIS provides direct searching for information. To provide WAIS access, a computer site must first use special software to create an index of its files as a database, then set up a WAIS server to provide access to the database.

To search the database, you list the keywords you want to search for, and the WAIS client will display a list of the files that match your query in descending order by the number of postings. From this list you can request the files you want. WAIS access is very useful for retrieving bibliographic information such as library catalogs, or full-text data such as legal decisions or technical reports.

More and more *Campus Wide Information Servers* (CWIS) are also accessible on the Internet. These systems provide information about universities, such as course descriptions, timetables, faculty and staff, calendars of events, job opportunities, publications, annual reports, and so on.

TELNET

Telnet is a facility that enables you to treat a remote computer as your own—to log onto it and manipulate and retrieve data. To use it, you provide the name of the host computer to which you want to connect. Publicly available computer services often prompt you with the correct log-in sequence, or you can find these in some of the guides in Figure 21–1. Once Telnet has set up the connection, it sends your keystrokes and displays the characters the computer sends back. Telnet is most often used to access resources provided by institutions, such as their CWIS or library catalog.

THE WORLD WIDE WEB

The World Wide Web (WWW) originated in 1989 in Switzerland at CERN, the European Laboratory for Particle Physics. A project was mounted to merge the techniques of information networks with hyperlinked text; the result was the Web. The development of the Web has now been taken over by INRIA, the French national institute in computer science and control.

To get into the Web, you need special client or *browser* software. The Web did not really take off until early 1993 when the U.S. National Center for Supercomputer Applications released the browser *Mosaic*. Now there are many other browsers available. The two best known are *Netscape* and Microsoft's *Internet Explorer*. Both are graphical browsers that can provide access to text, images, sound, and video. Computers that have character-based, rather than image-based, terminals can gain access to the Web using *Lynx*.

Each Website has a *homepage*, or starting screen, which provides an overview of its contents. The homepage may concentrate on a particular topic or organization. Figure

21–2 indicates the types of resources you might find listed on an organization's homepage.

Words or images that are underlined or highlighted provide hyperlinked access to related information, on the same Website or anywhere else on the Web. As a user, you are virtually unaware that by clicking on a word or image on one screen, you may be moving from one computer to another.

To provide hyperlinked access to Web documents, the providers must first format the words and images to be linked using *HyperText Markup Language* (*HTML*). Information is transferred between computers using *HyperText Transfer Protocol* (*HTTP*). *Uniform Resource Locators* (*URLs*) uniquely identify each system or resource on the Internet. A URL indicates the type of resource ("http" for WWW documents, "ftp" for FTP servers, and so on), the address of the computer where the resource is located, and the hierarchical location of the resource within that computer system.

When you access a site, you may get a message asking if you can be sent a *cookie*. This is a piece of information sent by a server to a browser. The browser software is expected to save it and send it back to the server when the browser makes additional requests from the server.

Your browser may store the HTML codes and graphics for the Web pages you access in a *cache* on your hard disk. This means that when you go back to a page it can be accessed from the disk rather than downloading it again from the Web, which is much faster. If it has been a while since you last accessed the page, however, the contents may have been changed. You can check by clicking on the "Reload" or "Refresh" button on your screen.

Figure 21–2 Set-up of a typical homepage for an institution or organization.

Home page $\longrightarrow$	Clicks to the $\longrightarrow$ next menu	Leads to the information itself
Frequently asked questions		Series of questions and answers
What's new	Headlines	Media releases
Events and activities	Speakers, programs, tours, conferences, and exhibitions	Time, date, place, cost, and description of events
Resources	Published books, magazines, reports	Bibliographic descriptions, abstracts, or full text
Links	Websites, FTP, e-mail discussion lists, and newsgroups	URLs or e-mail addresses, with annotations
Members	Officers, directory of members	Photographs, biographies, contact details
Membership		Benefits, fees, and how to join

GOOD PLACES TO START A WWW SEARCH

If you're a newcomer to the Web, there are several good places to start. Most university libraries have a hyperlinked list of Internet resources. If yours doesn't, try the Library of Congress "Explore the Internet" page (lcweb.loc.gov/global/explore.html), which links to a wide range of search tools, government resources, and sites where you can learn more about the Internet. The All-in-One Search Page (allonesearch.com) lists over 400 of the Internet's search engines, databases, indexes, and directories in a single site.

Just as you used catalogs, indexes, abstracting journals, and bibliographies to search your library's collection, you can use a *search engine* to search the Web. Search engines are of three types: subject directories, text-indexing search tools, and metasearch engines. These types are each explained in more detail below.

These search engines build up indexes from a variety of sources: some from the titles of Web pages, some from the full Website contents, and some from other indexes and directories. Each day, there are programs called *spiders*, *robots*, or *crawlers* that scan the Web looking for new URLs.

Once you start using a range of search engines, you'll find that they differ from each other. These differences include (University of Canberra, 1999):

- Number and currency of sites searched and frequency of additions
- Ease of use, including availability of help screens
- Range and sophistication of search options
- Speed of search
- Display features for results
- Number and relevance of items retrieved.

There are now a number of books and Websites that describe and compare the various search engines.

Subject Directories

Yahoo! is the best known of the subject directories and operates using menu-driven searching (see Chapter 2), often called subject tree or hierarchical searching. *Yahoo!* provides access to the Web by organizing its list of sites by broad topics, then subtopics, then narrower topics within these subtopics, and so on. To find what you are after, say information on the Rorschach Inkblot Test for psychology, you would need to follow the menu pathway: Social science → Psychology → Research → Tests and experiments → Rorschach Inkblot Test.

Another less centralized subject directory is the *WWW Virtual Library* (vlib.org). It started at CERN in 1991 in order to provide some order to the Web, and has been managed by the W3 Consortium since 1996. Volunteers all over the world now keep tabs on more than 270 different subject areas.

Text-indexing Search Tools

The majority of search engines are text-indexing search tools, and several important ones are listed in Figure 21–3. They provide keyword searching using a range of logical operators (see Chapter 10), proximity connectors (see Chapter 19), and other features. As occurs with CD-ROM and online databases, there is inconsistency in how these are applied. For example, an AND operation may occur by default (that is, if two or more terms are entered, the AND operation is assumed), it may require a plus sign between each of the terms, it may require an "AND" between each of the terms, or it may require that "AND" be selected from a pull-down box.

The results of searches are generally listed in order of most likely relevance, based on the number of search terms found on the page, where they are located, and how close

Figure 21–3 Important search engines on the World Wide Web.

Text-indexing search tools	URL	Characteristics
AltaVista	altavista.com	Large, fast. Covers Web and Usenet. Can search with words and phrases, logical operators, and proximity connector NEAR. Good search-refining tools.
Excite	excite.com	Covers Web, Usenet, and classified ads. Can search by concept and keyword using logical operators. Ranks relevance by confidence percentile.
Hotbot	hotbot.com	One of the largest databases. Covers Web. Can search by keyword in simple, modified, and expert searches using logical operators in pull-down boxes, date, or media types. Relevance scoring by words in title and length of document.
Infoseek	infoseek.go.com	Fast, reliable. Covers Web, Usenet, some databases. Can search by keywords, phrases, + and – as logical operators. Results presented as numerical score based on word frequency.
Lycos	lycos.com	Covers Web, Usenet, news, and stocks. Basic and advanced search options, including all logical operators. Can search on image and sound files.

Metasearch engines	URL	
Dogpile	dogpile.com	
Mamma	mamma.com	
Metacrawler	go2net.com	
Savvysearch	savvysearch.com	

they are to each other. Most text-indexing search tools have advanced options to carry out more sophisticated searches or to limit searches that retrieve too much. These are usually explained on help screens accessible from the home page.

Metasearch Engines

Metasearch engines enable you to search several of the search engines together at the same time using a single format. Several are listed in Figure 21–3. For example, when *Dogpile* carries out a search of the Web, it covers *Yahoo!*, *Lycos*, *InfoSeek*, *Excite*, *AltaVista*, and several other search engines—13 in all.

The advantage of using a metasearch engine is that this saves you from having to learn the individual idiosyncrasies of each of the other search engines. The disadvantages are that it can take longer because of the larger number of sites being searched; and although there may be more results, there may well be a larger proportion that are not relevant.

IN CONCLUSION

Trained as a librarian, I find the Web untidy. Libraries are organized according to established principles, and if you understand them, you can find your way around any library. The Web has protocols for data transfer, but beyond that, there's inconsistency.

Sometimes you may have difficulty finding your way back to the same place twice, although the *bookmark* facility allows you to mark a spot so that you can return directly to it. Sometimes you can end up at the same place (that is, being presented with the same place on a menu) not once or twice but multiple times, even when you have already been there and do not want to return. This is because the Web has so much built-in redundancy. *Netscape* and other browsers help you to avoid this problem by changing the color of the links you have already visited.

The Internet is still in its adolescence, but already some of the early means of access such as Gopher, Veronica, and Archie are being superseded. New means of access make it simpler for users to find their way around. The *Virtual Reality Modeling Language* (*VRML*), for example, is a new standard on the Web that enables users to explore a three-dimensional environment that mimics the real world. *Java* goes a step further: it animates the static VRML images and enables them to move.

RealAudio enables users equipped with multimedia computers and voice-grade telephone lines to browse, select, and play back audio content on demand, in real time, such as live broadcasts of radio programs. Or you can play and download music using the *MP3* file format.

In the meantime, it is important for you to feel at home on the Internet. The only way to do this is to roam it widely and find out what information sources are there in order to become more selective in which ones you access and how you access them.

More importantly, you need to become selective in deciding whether the Internet is even your best source for answering a query. Just because information is online, it may not be in a form that is the most up-to-date, the easiest to acquire, or the quickest to use. In many cases a printed source or a telephone call may be better, faster, and cheaper.

As the Librarian of Congress, James Billington, has written (1996: 3): "I am haunted by the thought that all this miscellaneous, unsorted, unverified, constantly changing information on the Internet may inundate knowledge, may move us back down the evolutionary chain from knowledge to information, from information to raw data."

A recent article (Dynamic Learning Consortium, 1996) published on the Web itself echoed this sentiment: "Information is only a low-level type of knowledge, and too much information of doubtful stability, reliability, or relevance ("infoglut") actually impairs real learning."

Despite these comments, the next century will surely bring added opportunities to broaden our range of inquiry and consequently our knowledge. The Internet can be useful if we remember, as Paul Gilster suggests (1997: 259), "to examine content with a mind honed on rationality and skepticism."

Appendix 1

Tips for Precision Searching
in Alphabetical Lists

WORD-BY-WORD VS. LETTER-BY-LETTER FILING

There are two different ways of filing alphabetically that can dramatically alter the sequence in which entries are listed. In word-by-word filing, blanks precede the letter "A" in alphabetical order. In letter-by-letter filing, blanks are ignored completely and words are treated as if they were compressed. Examples are shown below:

Word-by-word	Equivalent to	Letter-by-letter	Equivalent to
Ne Win (1911–)	ne	Newcastle	newca
New England	new e	Newcombe, John (1944–)	newco
New Guinea	new g	New England	newe
New Testament	new t	New Guinea	newg
Newcastle	newca	Ne Win (1911–)	newi
Newcombe, John (1944–)	newco	Newman, Paul (1925–)	newm
Newman, Paul (1925–)	newm	Newt	newt
Newt	newt	New Testament	newte

PUNCTUATION MARKS

Punctuation marks may be ignored completely, like blanks in letter-by-letter filing; or they may be treated as if they were blanks, and the letter(s) preceding them treated as if they were separate words, as in word-by-word filing. This may place some materials in seemingly odd places. For example, U.N.E.S.C.O. may be in the "U blanks," but "Unesco" in its normal place in alphabetical order.

Particularly for filing done by computer, some punctuation marks may take precedence over others. Ampersands may or may not be treated as if they were spelled out. Some variations are shown below:

Punctuation Ignored, Letter-by-letter Filing

A.B.C. Commission	= abccom
ABC Corporation	= abccor
Ab, Charles	= abch
A & B Company	= abco

Punctuation Treated as Blanks, Ampersand Spelled Out, Word-by-word Filing

A & B Company	= a a
A.B.C. Commission	= a b
Ab, Charles	= ab
ABC Corporation	= abc

Periods Precede All Other Punctuation Treated Equally Which Precede Letters of the Alphabet, Letter-by-letter Filing

A.B.C. Commission	= a.
A & B Company	= a&
Ab, Charles	= ab,
ABC Corporation	= abc

ARTICLES AND PREPOSITIONS

Articles ("a," "an," and "the") are usually ignored in alphabetizing when they are the first words in headings. The same rule applies to articles in foreign languages: for example, "le," "la," and "les" in French; "der," "die," and "das" in German; "el," "la," "los," and "las" in Spanish; and so on. Occasionally these foreign articles are used for alphabetizing in English language sources such as telephone directories. For example, La Boheme Cafe would appear under the letter "L," not "B."

Articles are usually included in determining alphabetical order when they appear internally in headings. For example, "Indians of Southwest Mexico" (equivalent to "indians of s") would precede "Indians of the Southwest" (equivalent to "indians of t").

Sometimes, especially in lists of medical and scientific serials, articles and prepositions (for example, "of," "in," or "on") are ignored and only the substantive words are included. In this case, *Journal of the Medical Society* (equivalent to "journal m") would precede *Journal of Surgical Procedures* (equivalent to "journal s").

INITIALISMS, ABBREVIATIONS, AND ACRONYMS

Initialisms, abbreviations, and acronyms may be treated in several ways. They may appear at the beginning of each letter of the alphabet, before normal words starting with that letter; they may be treated as if spelled out in full; or they may be treated as if they were words in their own right and filed accordingly. Examples are shown below.

Acronyms first, abbreviations spelled out	Acronyms interspersed, abbreviations spelled out	Treated as they appear
MCG	Mayan Indians	Mayan Indians
MP	MCG	MCG
Mayan Indians	Mr Juicy	Mother Hubbard
Mr Juicy	Mother Hubbard	MP
Mother Hubbard	Mt Kosciusko	Mr Juicy
Mt Kosciusko	MP	Mt Kosciusko

"MAC" AND "MC"

Some sources list names beginning with "Mac" or "Mc" exactly as they are spelled, while others treat "Mc" as though spelled "Mac":

As spelled	Mc as Mac
MacArthur, Douglas	MacArthur, Douglas
Mackerras, Sir Charles	McCartney, Paul
Mann, Thomas	Mackerras, Sir Charles
McCartney, Paul	McLuhan, Marshall
McLuhan, Marshall	Mann, Thomas

Still others list "Mac" and "Mc" together, either at the beginning of the "M's"; or after "Mab" but before all the other words or names that begin with "Mac," such as "Macedonia" and "machinery."

NUMBERS

Numbers are usually filed as if spelled out: 100 as "one hundred," 2,001 as "two thousand and one," and 3rd as "third". There are exceptions, however. In some sources, all the numbers may come together at the very beginning (before "A") or at the very end (after "Z"), listed in numerical rather than alphabetical order.

Some computer filing also puts all those numbers starting with 1 before all those starting with 2 before all those starting with 3 and so on. You might thus find a list such as:

1 at a time
10
101 Dalmatians
2 by 2
2001, A Space Odyssey

SPELLING

British and American spellings of the same word are generally treated as spelled. This may separate the same word quite dramatically (for example, "esophagus" and "oesophagus"). The following combinations can cause problems: e/ae, as in encyclopedia/encyclopaedia; e/oe, as in ameba/amoeba; er/re, as in center/centre; iz/is, as in organization/organisation; f/ph, as in sulfur/sulphur; or/our, as in harbor/harbour; and l/ll, as in labeling/labelling. Note also hiccup/hiccough.

Names pronounced the same way but spelled differently can also cause problems—for example Smith and Smyth, or Johnston and Johnstone.

NAMES

Normal practice is to alphabetize people's names listing the surname first, followed by the first name. This holds true for Asian names, but the surname may be first already; for example, Mao Tse-tung is filed by "Mao," not "Tse-tung." There may, however, be other intervening words as well, such as honorifics; for example, Dato' seri Haji Mohd Najib Bin Tun Haji Abdul Razak is filed by "Mohd."

For compound surnames, alphabetization is by the first of the two names. Peter Fonda-Bonardi is thus alphabetized by "Fonda", not "Bonardi." Terms of honor and address such as "Dame" or "Sir" are ignored when the entry heading begins with a surname.

Royalty and saints are usually listed by their first names, with numerical ordering for those with the same names:

Francis I (1494–1547) King of France
Francis II (1544–60) King of France
Francis Joseph (1830–1916) Emperor of Austria
Francis of Assisi, St

Corporate bodies such as companies, hospitals, and schools that have been named after people are usually alphabetized by the full name as it is known. The William Penn High School, for example, would be listed by "William," even though William Penn himself would be listed by "Penn, William."

ORDER OF ENTRIES FOR THE SAME WORD

When the same word or combination of words is used as the heading for different categories of entries, they may all be interspersed, or sometimes certain categories may come before others.

Information sources written or edited by a person may, for example, precede all sources written about a person. Personal surnames may be filed together, followed by compound surnames, and then all other entries also using that word, as shown below:

Stone, John
Stone, Peter
Stone-Bissell, Jason
Stone archways
Stone Masons Association

SUBDIVISIONS OF HEADINGS

The punctuation used to indicate a subdivision of a heading may be grouped, or it may be interspersed with other types of punctuation as well as headings incorporating the same term. For example:

Terms and punctuation grouped	Terms and punctuation interspersed
Engineering	Engineering
Engineering, civil	Engineering as a profession
Engineering, electrical	Engineering—Australia
Engineering, mechanical	Engineering, civil
Engineering—Australia	Engineering, electrical
Engineering—Japan	Engineering—Japan
Engineering as a profession	Engineering, mechanical

Headings such as histories of particular countries are sometimes filed chronologically rather than alphabetically.

Appendix 2

Terminology Related to the Book

Terminology related to the book is given here not in alphabetical order, but in the order in which the parts are generally encountered. Familiar terms (cover, spine, title, pages, dedication, and so on) have not been included.

Dust jacket: illustrated wrapper that protects a book, usually incorporating the title, a "blurb" promoting the contents, and information about the author.

Cover title: title that appears on the cover of a book, which may differ from the title on the title page. The cover title may be shorter or more striking, to fit in with the cover design.

End papers: papers pasted to the inside covers to help keep a book firmly in its binding. They may be plain or feature maps or illustrations.

Leaf: a unit comprising two printed pages of a book, one on each side. The term is also applied to blank or illustrated pages.

Recto: front or righthand page, always odd-numbered. The title page, preface, table of contents, and the first page of the first chapter are usually rectos.

Verso: overleaf or lefthand page, always even-numbered. Copyright pages are usually versos.

Frontispiece: an illustrated leaf preceding the title page of a book.

Title page: the recto page near the front of a book on which are usually printed its title, the author's name, the edition (if other than the first), the publisher's name, and the place of publication.

Subtitle: a secondary or subordinate part of a title.

Series title: collective title given to monographs in a series.

Edition: all the copies of a book printed from one set of printing plates. The same or updated text, printed from a different set of plates, is a different edition. Editions that contain changes, new material, or information bringing the text up-to-date are generally numbered (2nd, 3rd, and so on) or described as new or revised editions.

Publisher: person, body, or firm responsible for the production of a book, and often for its distribution.

Place of publication: location of the publishing house from which a book emanated.

Imprint: the publisher, place, and date of publication of a book, taken together.

Copyright page: the verso of a title page, on which the date of publication, copyright date, number of reprints or impressions, International Standard Book Number, and Cataloging-in-Publication data are usually indicated.

Date of publication: the date when that edition of a book was published.

Copyright date: the date from which the author or agent has protected his or her rights to the ownership of the text, as indicated by the symbol "©." The copyright date is often related to the first edition of a book.

Impression or reprint: more copies of a particular edition of a book printed from the same set of printing plates used previously. (Technically, a reprint is made from new, but nearly identical, plates with only minor errors corrected.)

International Standard Book Number (*ISBN*): a unique number assigned to each book, based on country of publication and publisher.

Cataloging-in-Publication (*CIP*): the data elements related to a book, set out in a bibliographic description similar to that found in a library catalog.

Table of contents: list of chapter headings in sequential order, with page numbers, immediately following a book's title or dedication page.

Introduction, preface, acknowledgments, and foreword: preliminary sections, usually paginated using Roman numerals, whose contents may indicate the author's or publisher's aims in creating the book, its scope or limitations, its intended audience, its relationship to previous editions, or the persons involved in research and publication.

Running title: a full or shortened title that is repeated at the top of each page throughout the book. The title of the book usually appears on the verso and the title of the chapter on the recto.

Plates: full-page illustrations printed on heavier paper, often bound together in sections.

Bibliography, references, or readings: list of information sources located at the end of each chapter or the end of the book, which the author consulted in writing the book or is suggesting to readers for further study.

Glossary: list of important technical, special, or foreign terms, with explanations or definitions, in alphabetical order.

Appendix: section containing supplementary information that does not fit easily into the main body of a book, such as detailed numerical data, tables, graphs, lists, examples, or samples.

Index: list of subjects, authors, geographic areas, or other features covered in a book, usually arranged alphabetically, with locations (usually page numbers). The index is normally found at the very back of a book.

Reference List

Anthes, Gary H. 1996. "Predicting the Future." *Computerworld.* (June 3).

Bassett, Ed. 1997. Interview with Margaret Chisholm (May 15).

Billington, James H. 1996. "A Technological Flood Requires Human Navigators." *American Libraries.* 27, no. 6 (June-July): 39–40.

Braun, Erin E., ed. 1998. *Gale Directory of Databases.* 2 vols. Detroit: Gale Research.

Breivik, Patricia Senn. 1991. "Information Literacy." *Bulletin of the Medical Library Association.* 79, no. 2 (April): 226–29.

Breivik, Patricia Senn and E. Gordon Gee. 1989. *Information Literacy: Revolution in the Library.* New York: American Council on Education/Macmillan.

Dynamic Learning Consortium. 1996. "Education for the Twenty-first Century." (March 3) www.transform.org.transform/dic/rapids/p6main.html.

Finlay, Matthew, ed. 1993. *The CD-ROM Directory 1994, with Multimedia CD's.* Intl. 11th ed. London: TFPL Publishing.

Follett, Wilson. 1962. "Sabotage in Springfield: Webster's Third Edition." *The Atlantic.* 209, no. 1 (January): 73–79.

Gilster, Paul. 1997. *Digital Literacy.* New York: John Wiley.

Godden, Jean. 1997. Interview with Margaret Chisholm (May 9).

Katz, William A. 1992. *Introduction to Reference Work: Vol. I, Basic Information Sources.* 6th ed. New York: McGraw-Hill.

Landau, Herbert B., Jerome T. Maddock, F. Floyd Shoemaker, and Joseph G. Costello. 1982. "An Information Transfer Model to Define Information Users and Outputs with Specific Application to Environmental Technology." *Journal of the American Society for Information Science.* 33, no. 2 (March): 82–91.

Lovett, Neil. 1977. "You Are What You Say in the Australian Dictionary." *National Times.* (April 25–30): 18–19.

Redmond, Ron. 1997. Interview with Margaret Chisholm (May 12).

Suchowski, Amy R., ed. 1998. *CD-ROMs in Print*. 12th ed. Detroit: Gale Research.

Times Atlas of the World. 1992. Comprehensive ed. London: Times Books.

Underwood, Douglas. 1997. Interview with Margaret Chisholm (May 13).

University of Canberra, Division of Information Management and Tourism. 1999. "Information Access. Module 4.4 Searching the Web: A Brief Guide." (April 11), teaching.canberra.edu.au:8900/SCRIPT? LIS5194/scripts.students/serve_page?882560079+Searchind.html.

Who's Who. 1991. 143rd ed. London: A & C Black.

Who's Who in America. 1997. 51st ed. New Providence, New Jersey: Marquis.

Williams, Martha E. 1998. "The State of Databases Today, 1998": xvii–xxix. *Gale Directory of Databases* Vol. 1. Detroit: Gale Research.

Wolff, Geoffrey. 1974. "Britannica 3, History of." *The Atlantic*. 233, no. 6 (June): 37–47.

Resource Index

This index includes information sources in print and electronic form, including databases and Internet homepages. It uses word-by-word filing, ignores punctuation and intersperses acronyms with other words.

Topic Index

This index uses word-by-word filing, ignores punctuation and intersperses acronyms with other words. For titles of publications, databases and Internet sites, see the Resource Index.

About the Authors

Dr Nancy Lane is the communications manager and development officer for the Australian Academy of Science. She has previously been a director of library and information science schools at the University of Canberra in the Australian Capital Territory and Curtin University in Perth, Western Australia. She has published several books and articles on information technology and its applications.

Dr Margaret Chisholm was the director of the Graduate School of Library and Information Science at the University of Washington. She served as president of the American Library Association, and was a consultant to the Guadalajara and Zimbabwe book fairs and the Caribbean library association. Most recently she taught creative writing courses for passengers aboard the *Island Princess* cruise ship.

Carolyn Mateer was the head of Reference and Research Services at the University of Washington. She has worked for Barnes and Noble, and is particularly interested in Latin American and Australian literature. She has also taught aboard the *Island Princess*.